Mastering the Case Analysis

The MBA Guide to Management, Marketing, and Strategic Consulting Case Interviews

Alexander Chernev

2007 Edition

Mastering the Case Analysis: The MBA Guide to Management, Marketing, and Strategic Consulting Case Interviews

Third Edition

ISBN 0-9763061-7-4

www.InterviewToolbox.com

Published by Brightstar Media, Inc.

Printed in USA

Table of Contents

Preface

Case analysis is an integral part of many consulting, management, and marketing interviews. To be successful in a case interview, you must demonstrate an ability to systematically solve business problems. In reality, however, very few candidates apply a systematic approach to case analysis. Moreover, of those who try to be systematic in their analyses, many end up force-fitting a few familiar frameworks to solve unrelated business problems – one of the most common mistakes in case analysis. This occurs because candidates tend to use frameworks without an in-depth understanding of their limitations and areas of applicability. This problem is further exacerbated by the lack of universal frameworks for case analysis. Indeed, most of the existing business frameworks have been created to illustrate a particular concept and/or theory rather than to be used as a tool for solving diverse business problems. To address this problem, this book introduces a comprehensive approach to provide an algorithm for management, marketing, and strategic consulting case analysis.

A popular strategy used to prepare for case interviews is to read numerous transcripts of real interviews. While familiarizing yourself with a few specific examples of case interviews is definitely helpful, one of the biggest problems with relying exclusively on transcripts is that it is virtually impossible to prepare in advance an answer for all the possible questions you might be asked during the interview. Therefore, instead of simply offering transcripts from past interviews, this book introduces a systematic approach to business problem-solving that may be applied beyond the course of the interview to solve real business problems. The problem-solving approach presented in this book might appear more complex than other case analysis guides. This complexity is not self-serving; it reflects the complex nature of business problems facing companies in today's dynamic marketplace.

When preparing for case interviews, it is important to keep in mind that case analysis is not something that can be learned overnight. This should not be a surprise: Do you really think that consulting companies will pay somebody a six-digit salary based on knowledge that can be acquired by reading a single book overnight? The goal of this book, therefore, is to help you streamline the knowledge you have readily accumulated in your prior professional and academic experience in a format commonly used in job interviews.

Mastering the Case Analysis: The MBA Guide to Management, Marketing, and Strategic Consulting Case Interviews offers a systematic approach to analyzing business cases typically given in the interview context. This book is organized in five chapters. The first chapter delivers a comprehensive analysis of the case interview process and offers in-depth insights on how to develop a successful case interview strategy. The second chapter introduces an integrative framework for solving business problems typically used in case interviews. The third chapter reviews the most common case problems given in an interview context and identifies a set of general solution strategies. The last two chapters are a succinct reference guide offering an overview of the key concepts and frameworks commonly used in case analysis.

Part I: Mastering the Case Analysis

Chapter 1: The Case Interview

1.1. The Interview Process

The case analysis is an integral part of many consulting, management, and marketing interviews. To master the case analysis, it is important to first understand the role of case analysis as a part of the interview process.

From a structural standpoint, the interview consists of several parts. It starts with an introduction, followed by questions about your personal experience and often by a case analysis. Most interviewers also provide candidates an opportunity to ask questions about the company. The interview usually concludes with a closure in which the candidate highlights his/her value to the interviewing company and establishes a follow-up procedure (Figure 1.1). Each of these interview components are discussed in more detail below.

Figure 1.1. The Interview Process

- *Introduction.* Most interviews begin with an introduction in which the interviewer and the candidate greet one another and exchange a few ice-breaking comments. It is also common for the interviewer to offer a beverage (water, coffee, tea, soda). The interview is then commonly initiated with an open-ended general question of the "tell me about yourself" type – a question that also serves as the transition to the personal experience portion of the interview.
- *The Personal Experience Interview.* The personal experience interview (also referred to as a behavioral interview) aims to reveal candidates' core skills, knowledge, and their fit with the company. This part of the interview usually involves asking the candidate to provide examples of a situation in which he/she has demonstrated the set of skills that is important to the recruiting company.
- *Case Analysis.* Case interviews test a candidate's ability to solve problems on the spot. It demonstrates a candidate's agility in navigating the issues in search of the most logical solution. As an additional benefit, the interactive nature of the case interview adds a dynamic dimension to understanding a candidate's personality and allows better

evaluation of the fit between the candidate and the interviewer's company.

- *The Candidate's Questions.* Many recruiters also allow candidates to ask questions about both the company and the job. Candidates' questions are an integral part of the interview because they are usually a good indicator of what is really important to a given candidate and are thus often used to evaluate his/her fit with the company's goals and value system.
- *Closure.* Closing the interview gives candidates the option to summarize their unique value proposition and reiterate their interest in the company.

1.2. The Case Interview

Recruiters seek to hire candidates who can add value to their company. The interviewer's goal, therefore, is to identify candidates whose value proposition best fits the needs of the organization and who have the highest potential to create value for the company. In this context, your success in the interview is determined by the degree to which your value proportion fits the company's needs.

Being a successful manager requires the ability to deal creatively with complex problems and reach logical conclusions based on the available facts within a short timeframe. Because no particular background or set of qualifications prepares candidates for that, many companies have come to rely on the case analysis approach as an integral part of the interview process.

Case analysis involves two types of problems: business cases and brainteasers. Business cases deal with business problems such as profitability, market share, mergers and acquisitions, new product launch decisions, etc. Brainteasers, in contrast, deal with logical problems across different contexts. These two types of cases are discussed in more detail in the following sections.

1.3. Business Cases

1.3.1. Business Case Basics

Case analysis examines a candidate's approach to a complex situation and tests skills and competencies to identify and solve complex problems. Case analysis places particular emphasis on factors that are more difficult to test in the context of the traditional interview. These factors include logical reasoning and quantitative analysis (analytical skills), creative problem solving (creativity), the ability to clearly express your point of view (communication skills), and professional poise and ability to perform under pressure (management skills).

In a case interview, the candidate is introduced to a particular business scenario and asked to analyze the situation and offer a solution. The interview proceeds as an open dialogue between the interviewer and the candidate, during which time the candidate's goal is to identify the source of the problem and recommend a solution.

The key issue to keep in mind is that case analysis is not about the solution per se; it is about how you arrive at that solution. Rather than looking for one specific answer, interviewers are trying to understand how you think. In this context, the interviewer is more interested in your assumptions, your selection of a framework, and the quality of your reasoning rather than your ability to arrive at the "right answer" (which, as a matter of fact, often does not exist).

A good strategy to use in approaching case analysis is to think of the interview as a problem-solving task in which you work through hypothetical business problems. Try to forget that this is an interview and think as of it as a consulting assignment in which the interviewer is the client. Your goal should be to solve your client's problem rather than guess at the "right" answer. Remember that the interviewer's goal is to hire a person who will be solving business problems on a day-to-day basis and, hence, needs to feel comfortable with the process.

Business cases can be presented in one of two formats: oral and written. These two formats are discussed in more detail below.

Oral cases are presented in an interactive manner. They offer very little information up front and leave it up to the candidate to uncover the case specifics. Oral cases are very popular among recruiters, especially during the early rounds of interviews, because they provide excellent insights into candidates' ability to identify the relevant information, decision processes, and interpersonal skills. Common types of business cases include advising a client about an acquisition, responding to a competitive move by another company in the industry, and evaluating opportunities for a new product introduction. Business problems are often phrased as "CEO questions" or "client questions." For example: "You are the CEO of a telecommunications company and your profits are falling despite the overall category growth. What do you do?" Or "You have been hired to advise a major consumer goods company that is considering launching a new line of lunch cereals. How would you advise your client?"

In addition to the typical business problems, interviews can involve behavioral cases that deal with relationship-building and team-management issues. A common behavioral case involves a client project in which something has gone wrong, and the goal is to resolve the problem, control the damage, and deal with the team and/or the client. The candidate might be asked to explain what he/she would do to resolve the situation or, alternatively, he/she might be asked to role-play the interaction.

Written cases are usually several pages long and are accompanied by data figures that contain supplemental information. Candidates are usually given time to read the case and prepare for a discussion. Written cases offer insights into a candidate's ability for logical reasoning and quantitative skills, as well as the ability to interpret complex data patterns. An important part of written case analysis involves interpreting different data patterns, usually presented in the form of a chart and/or a table. The goal is to assess candidates' ability to interpret data presented in different formats and their ability to derive conclusions from these data. This type of case is often used by recruiters during advanced rounds of the interview, although some consulting companies (e.g., Bain & Company) tend to use written cases during the early rounds as well.

Written cases can also be tested in a group context. In a group case analysis, each of the candidates is given a written case and a set of specific questions to be answered. After reading the case, candidates take part in a group discussion in which they present their solution and comment on the solutions presented by other team members. Recruiters are looking for candidates who can present their own findings, integrate the input from other team members, and comment on the solutions presented by other team members. In this context, group interviews are a litmus test for a candidate's leadership abilities, interpersonal skills, and collaborative spirit.

1.3.2. Using Frameworks in Case Analysis

The increasing complexity of the business processes within and across companies calls for a systematic approach to structuring the relevant information in a format that facilitates managerial decision making. Such a systematic attempt to provide a logical structure for organizing complex information can best be achieved using frameworks.

Frameworks are the cornerstones of business analysis because they offer a simplified description of complex processes and provide a general solution to a variety of industry-specific problems. Frameworks streamline the decision process by providing managers with a common view on how to frame the problem, with a universal approach to identifying alternative solutions and a shared vocabulary to discuss the issues. Because of their level of generality, frameworks rarely offer solutions to specific business problems. Instead, they provide a general algorithm which, when applied to a specific scenario, allows managers to identify the optimal solution.

Employing a framework for solving business problems is vital for successful case analysis. Recruiting companies are not particularly interested in the candidate's solution to the problem at hand; instead, they are interested in this candidate's ability to apply a systematic approach to solving diverse business problems. Yet, the selection and use of frameworks is one of the most common mistakes candidates make. Because of its complexity, the issue of using frameworks in case analysis is addressed in more detail in Chapters 2 and 3.

1.4. Brainteaser Cases

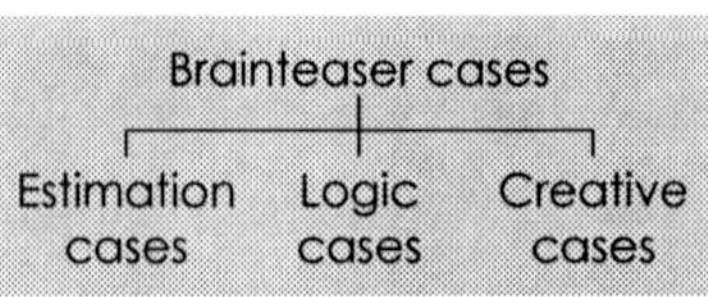

Brainteaser questions seek to directly test a candidate's creative problem-solving and logical reasoning skills. While not all interviewers use brainteasers, they are very common among management consulting and software companies. Unlike traditional business cases, brainteasers are usually abstract questions describing a specific (often non-business) problem. Although some questions might require certain factual knowledge, most brainteasers are self-contained logical tasks. There are three main types of brainteasers: (1) estimation cases (e.g., How many piano tuners are there in the world?), (2) logical cases (e.g., Why do Coke cans have an indentation on the bottom?), and (3) creative cases (e.g., How would you move Mount Fuji?). These three types of brainteasers are described in more detail in the following sections.

1.4.1. Estimation Questions

The popularity of estimation cases in management consulting interviews stems from the fact that these questions are not only easy to create, discuss, and evaluate, but also that they are representative of the type of problems managers and consultants face in their day-to-day work. Estimation questions typically require both logical deduction and quantitative skills. Their goal is not to test factual knowledge but, instead, to observe the candidate's approach to problem solving. In this context, the answer, per se, is often irrelevant; what counts is the process of arriving at the answer.

Estimation cases can vary from market-sizing problems in which the candidate has to determine the size of a particular market (e.g., What is the size of the market for the Segway human transporter?) to estimating physical factors such as weight and volume (e.g., How much does the moon weigh?). Additional examples of estimation questions and solution strategies are given in Appendix A.

Estimating questions can sometimes be part of a more comprehensive case analysis. To illustrate, the answer to the question of whether a company should launch a new product largely depends on the size of the potential market.

While each estimation question is likely to have its own unique set of solutions, two general approaches to estimation questions can be identified: analysis and analogy.

Estimation by analysis involves breaking down the object into smaller parts and estimating each part individually. For example, in the case of estimating the weight of an airplane, one might break down the problem into a series of more specific tasks such as estimating the weight of the different parts of the airplane: the body, engines, fuel, luggage, passengers, etc.

Estimation by analogy involves comparing the estimated object to a similar object with known parameters. To illustrate, when asked to estimate the number of car batteries sold annually in the United States, one can use the number of total car sales to arrive at the answer.

Estimation cases might require certain factual knowledge to derive the final answer (e.g., the size of the U.S. population, formulas to calculate the volume/weight of an object, etc.). Some of the key statistics relevant to solving estimation cases are given in Appendix B.

Knowing the facts helps, but it is not crucial. Remember, the goal of the interview is not to test whether you can get the "right" answer but to test your ability for logical reasoning. Therefore, if you do not have the necessary data readily available, describe the *process* you would use to solve the problem. In most cases, describing the algorithm is more important than running the actual calculations.

1.4.2. Logic Cases

Logic cases typically describe an abstract problem based on logical reasoning. The goal is to uncover the logical principle underlying the problem. Unlike estimation and creative questions, most logical problems have a unique solution. To illustrate, consider the following problem: Why do Coke cans have an indentation on the bottom? More examples of logic questions and solutions can be found in Appendix C.

1.4.3. Creative Cases

Creative cases are another form of brainteasers, and are very popular among companies in which creativity is paramount (e.g., software, design, product development, and advertising). By definition, creative cases can be about virtually anything. As an illustration, consider the following questions: How would you describe green to a blind person? How would you design a mobile phone for dogs? How would you design a restroom for a CEO? How would you develop a technology to grow straight bananas? How would you describe a pineapple to a person who has never seen one? How would you describe the business school of the future? These questions test a candidate's creativity and ability to think "outside of the box" in order to find an original solution to a non-trivial problem. An additional benefit of creative questions is that they lend themselves to interesting conversation that can provide further insights into the candidate's personality.

1.4.4. Preparing for a Brainteaser Interview

Because brainteaser questions lack a pre-set format, topic, and structure, one cannot really "prepare" for a brainteaser interview (which is one of the reasons that interviewers like these questions!). Practicing, however, can help you better articulate your decision process, improve your logical thinking, and help you develop your own strategy for approaching brainteaser questions.

1.5. Managing the Case Interview

The case interview typically starts with a brief description of a business scenario such as a client facing declining market share, eroding profit margins, or a new product introduction. Recruiters are not looking for candidates who happen to know the right answer and "crack the case" but rather for people who have a system that will allow them to solve *any* case. Indeed, even though each problem requires its own unique analysis, most companies believe that the process of analyzing various business problems has a common structure that carries across different scenarios. Therefore, when discussing the case, it is important to apply a logical, well-structured approach that enables you to reach a meaningful conclusion.

A common approach to case analysis includes four steps: clarify, structure, analyze, and conclude. These four steps to case analysis are logically connected (Figure 1.2). First, determine the situation, identify the problem, and verify the facts; next, develop and present a framework for analyzing the problem; then, apply the framework to analyze specific problems and derive effective solutions; finally, make a recommendation. These steps are outlined in more detail below.

Figure 1.2. Structuring the Case Interview

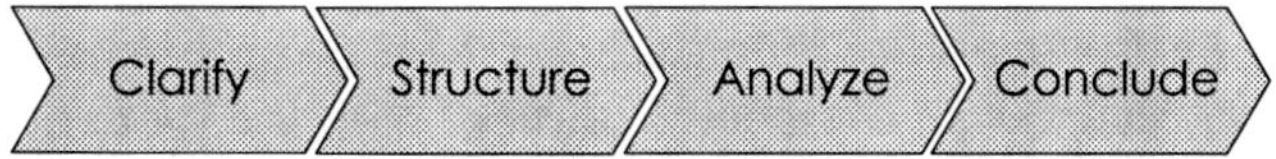

Clarify. The first step is to make sure that you understand the business scenario and the question you are being asked. In fact, one of the most common mistakes during a case interview is misunderstanding the question or answering the wrong question. Sometimes the interviewer will deliberately interject ambiguity into the problem as a part of the interview. Ask clarification questions if you are unclear about certain aspects of the case. A simple strategy used to begin case analysis is for the candidate to paraphrase the question to ensure that he/she understands the problem.

Structure. Structuring involves choosing an approach (framework) to solve the problem. It is a good idea to describe your overall approach and explain the logic used to address the problem. Try to find the appropriate framework to break the problem into separate issues, but do not force-fit a framework to the problem. Remember that your goal is not to showcase your knowledge of a particular framework but to demonstrate your ability to solve business problems. Frameworks are tools to help you organize your thinking; they are not the solution to the problem. It is a good idea to explain the reasons for selecting the framework you use and how you would go about applying the framework to the problem at hand. When given a complex problem, think broadly and be sure to cover all relevant issues rather than spending all your time on one particular issue (unless the interviewer asks you to do so).

Analyze. There are three basic components to a solid analysis: facts, assumptions, and logic.

- *Facts* are the cornerstones of your analysis and are used to derive your assumptions, logical conclusions, and proposed actions. Some of the facts may not be readily available and you will need to ask the interviewer to fill in the gaps. As a general rule, the shorter the case, the greater the likelihood that you will need to request additional information as you analyze the problem.

- *Assumptions* are necessary in order to fill in the missing facts. Making assumptions is a common practice in business analysis; the key is to ensure that your assumptions are realistic and clearly articulated. Use sensitivity analysis (e.g., compare an aggressive vs. a conservative scenario) when unsure about the validity of a particular assumption (e.g., market share growth, rate of new product adoption).

- *Logic* links the available information (facts and assumptions) to uncover new relationships (e.g., cause and effect), derive conclusions (e.g., if ... then...), and/or apply general business principles to the case at hand (e.g., an increase in price is likely to lead to a decrease in quantity sold). Break the problem into separate issues, address the issues one at a time, and state findings for each analysis. Remember that the interview is not about the outcome (i.e., getting the "right" answer) but about the process used in solving the problem. Walk the interviewer through your thought process and use visual aids (flowchart, matrix, bullet points) when possible (Appendix E).

Conclude. Conclude the case discussion by summarizing your logic and offering a recommendation that reflects your decision on how the company should address the situation described in the case. The proposed solution should be clear and based on your evaluation of facts, assumptions, and logic, rather than on unsubstantiated opinions. Link your recommendation back to the problem and identify how your solution will solve the problem. A useful format to close the case interview involves the following three steps: (1) restate the problem, (2) summarize the proposed solution, and (3) link the solution back to the problem by showing that this problem can be best solved by the proposed course of action.

Appendix A: Estimation Cases

Estimation cases are a form of brainteaser commonly used in interviews to test candidates' logical thinking and observe their quantitative skills. Examples of estimation questions utilized at management interviews are offered below.

Question: How many golf balls does it take to fill an Olympic swimming pool?

Solution A: The popular solution is to compare the volume of the swimming pool and the golf ball. Given that the pool is 50 meters x 25 meters x 3 meters, its volume is 3,750 cubic meters, or 228,837,667 cubic inches. The golf ball's volume is 2.48 cubic inches (the radius of the golf ball is 0.84 inches and the formula for measuring the volume of a sphere is: [4 x (Pi) x radius cubed] / 3). Given that the densest packing of spheres possible is 74%, it can be calculated that it takes 68.28 million golf balls to fill the pool. Note, however, that this solution requires very specific knowledge (e.g., the formula for measuring the volume of a sphere and the maximum density-packing coefficient) and, hence, is not readily applicable to most MBA interviews.

Solution B: An alternative (and more intuitive) solution does not require the knowledge of complex formulas. The size of an Olympic pool is 50 meters x 25 meters x 3 meters. The diameter of a golf ball is 1.68 inches or .0427 meters (1 inch = 2.54 centimeters). Therefore, it will take 685,000 golf balls to cover the bottom of the pool (1,171 x 585). The depth of the pool is 3 meters or 70 golf balls. Therefore, when golf balls are stacked by putting each layer precisely on top of one another, the swimming pool will accommodate approximately 47.95 million balls (685,000 x 70). Note, however that a greater efficiency can be achieved by shifting every other layer by 2.1 centimeters (half a golf ball). Assume that it will result in approximately 40% stacking efficiency (which can be illustrated by a simple drawing) – that is, instead of 70 layers of golf balls the pool will accommodate 98 layers (70 x 1.4). Therefore, the total amount of balls the swimming pool can accommodate is about 67.13 million (685,000 x 98).

Question: How many barbers are there in Chicago?

Solution: Chicago's population is close to 3 million → assume 50% are men → assume 6 haircuts per year → 9 million haircuts per year. Assume also that each haircut takes 30 minutes and the average barber works 8 hours a day, 5 days a week, 50 weeks a year (2 weeks vacation) → 4,000 haircuts per year. Therefore, there should be 2,250 barbers (assuming that all men get a haircut from a barber; if this is not the case, then the derived number is overestimated).

Additional Estimation Questions:

- Estimate the number of flashlights (fountain pens, cell phones, cars, etc.) sold each year in the United States (China, India, Germany, etc.).
- What is the size of the restaurant market in Chicago?
- How many computers are sold daily in China?
- What is the weight of a Boeing 747?
- How many gas stations (pay phones, restaurants) are there in Chicago?
- How would you go about estimating your competitor's budget for advertising/promotional/R&D expenses?
- How many car batteries are sold in the United States each year?
- How large is the market for hamburgers in United States?
- Estimate the market for laser printers in Russia.
- How many pounds of chocolate are consumed in the United States each year?

Appendix B: Useful Estimation Facts

U.S. Population*

Total Population	281
Male	138 (49%)
Female	143 (51%)
18 Years and Over	209 (74%)
65 Years and Over	35 (12%)
Total Households	105
Family Households	72 (68%)

*In Millions
Source: U.S. Census Bureau 2000

Largest Ten U.S. Cities*

1. New York, NY	8.0
2. Los Angeles, CA	3.7
3. Chicago, IL	2.9
4. Houston, TX	2.0
5. Philadelphia, PA	1.5
6. Phoenix, AZ	1.3
7. San Diego, CA	1.2
8. San Antonio, TX	1.1
9. Dallas, TX	1.2
10. San Jose, CA	0.9

* In Millions
Source: U.S. Census Bureau 2000

World Population*

China	1,200
India	984
Canada	30
Mexico	98
Germany	82
France	61
UK	60
Italy	58
Russia	143

* In Millions
Source: CIA – The World Fact Book 2005

Distances

New York to Chicago	719 miles
New York to Los Angeles	2,462 miles
New York to London	3471 miles
New York to Tokyo	6760 miles
New York to Beijing	6,847 miles
Around the Earth (at the equator)	24,902 miles

Miscellaneous Facts

Number of Cars in the U.S.*	204 million
Boeing 747-400	
- Empty weight	400,000 lbs
- Maximum takeoff weight	850,000 lbs

*Source: Bureau of Transportation Statistics

Appendix C: Logic Cases

Logic cases are a form of brainteasers commonly used in interviews to test candidates' ability to deal with abstract problems and to observe their problem-solving processes. Examples of logic problems given at management interviews are offered below.

Problem: Why are manhole covers round?

Solution A: A round cover cannot fall into a manhole, whereas square or rectangular ones can (e.g., if placed diagonally).

Solution B: Round manhole covers are more easily rolled down the street, if necessary.

Problem: Why do Coke cans have an indentation at the bottom?

Solution: Coke cans have this indentation in order to control can expansion so that, in case of pressure, it does not bulge in the opposite direction or at the sides. This would not allow the can to stand up normally and would make it less visually appealing.

Problem: You are in a room with three light switches. Each one controls one light bulb in the next room. Your goal is to figure out which switch controls which light bulb. You may flick only two switches and may enter into the light bulb room only once.

Solution: The key is to realize that a light bulb can also be tested by touch. Flick the first switch, wait for a few minutes, then turn it off and flick the second switch. Enter the light bulb room. The bulb that is on connects to the second switch. The warm light bulb is controlled by the first switch.

Problem: Consider a set of cards, each one having a letter on one side and a number on the other side. You are given a subset of four cards as follows (the upper side): D-K-3-7. You have to test the following rule: If a card has a D on one side, it has a 3 on the other side. You must decide which cards need to be turned over to determine whether this sample of cards is consistent with the rule.

Solution: The correct cards are D and 7 (although 90% of people pick D and 3). Seeing what is on the reverse of the 7 card can lead to disconfirming the rule if a D shows up (whereas seeing what is on the reverse of the 3 card cannot disconfirm the rule and is, hence, non-informative).[1]

Problem: Suppose that there are four possible kinds of objects: (1) an unhappy dodecahedron, (2) a happy dodecahedron, (3) an unhappy cube, and (4) a happy cube. Suppose, as well, that I have written down on a hidden piece of paper one of the attitudes (unhappy or happy) and one of the shapes (dodecahedron or cube). Now read the following rule carefully: An object is a GOKE if, and only if, it has either the attitude I have written down, or the shape I have written down, but not both. I will tell you that the unhappy dodecahedron is a GOKE. Which of the other objects, if any, is a GOKE?

Solution: A happy cube.[2]

Problem: A bat and a ball cost $1.10 in total. The bat costs $1 more than the ball. How much does the ball cost?

Solution: The ball costs five cents.[3]

Notes

[1] Wason, P. C. (1960), "On the Failure to Eliminate Hypotheses in a Conceptual Task," *Quarterly Journal of Experimental Psychology*, 12, 129-140.

[2] Ibid.

[3] Kahneman, Daniel (2003), "Maps of Bounded Rationality: Psychology for Behavioral Economics Dagger," *American Economic Review*, 93, 1449.

Appendix D: Winning Case Interview Strategies

Mastering the case analysis requires the ability to deal creatively with complex problems and reach logical conclusions in a short period of time, based on the available information. The case interview also calls for strong communication, teamwork, and general management skills, because the interactive nature of case analysis adds a dynamic dimension to the interview by letting the recruiter observe your poise, self-confidence, and communication skills under pressure. A set of winning strategies on how to manage these two aspects of the case interview are outlined below.

Solving the Case:

- Be sure you are answering the question you have been asked; ask questions if you are unsure about the details. Misunderstanding the question and answering the wrong question are some of the most common mistakes in a case interview.
- Remember that you are rarely given all the case information up front. You are expected to ask intelligent questions that will reveal the relevant information that is not readily available.
- Be systematic. Finish one key question and summarize the findings before you go on to the next. Step back periodically to summarize what you have learned thus far and how it relates to the problem you are trying to solve. Do not proceed in a haphazard fashion, jumping from one issue to another.
- Use frameworks creatively. Do not force-fit a familiar framework to a problem (one of the most common case analysis mistakes). The key is to use common sense.
- Always focus on the big picture; solve the problem without getting stuck in details. Prioritize issues. Begin with factors that are likely to have the greatest impact. There is no need to mention the framework you will be using by name; instead, explain the structure of your analysis so that the interviewer understands your thought process.
- Stay away from phrases like "as we learned in our strategy class..." and "the textbook says that..." to justify your decisions. You should be able to explain and justify the logic for your arguments on your own.

- Do not be afraid to think "outside the box." There is no box. Creativity and brainstorming may be just what the interviewer is seeking. Use business judgment, logic, and common sense.
- Identify the assumptions you are making to solve the problem. Explain the rationale for making these assumptions and their consistency with the facts of the case. Always clarify whether you are making assumptions of your own or restating the case facts.
- When possible, use visual aids to support your analysis. Use flowcharts to represent business processes (e.g., the value delivery process); use bullet points to identify different case points (e.g., facts, assumptions, and logical arguments); use matrixes to represent more complex relationships between factors with multiple levels (e.g., product-market matrix). Examples of visual aids commonly used in case analysis are given in Appendix E.
- When possible, use calculations to support your analysis. This is an opportunity to demonstrate your quantitative skills.

Interacting with the Interviewer:

- Listen carefully and take notes. Remember that you are not expected to have a ready solution to the case problem; take a moment to collect your thoughts.
- Think out loud. The interviewer wants to get to know your thought process, not just the solution. If you have rejected some alternatives, explain why so that the interviewer has a better understanding of your thought process.
- Structure your answer by explaining your strategy (framework) up front so that the interviewer knows what you are trying to do.
- Be confident, even if you do not know the answer to a specific question. It is important for the interviewer to understand that you know how to react if a client asks you something for which you do not know the answer.
- Remember that "cracking the case" does not mean finding the "right" answer (which rarely exists). It is all about how you analyze the problem.
- Interact with the interviewer. The case should be a dialogue, not a monologue.

- Be flexible in defending your point. The interviewer might disagree with you in order to test your reaction to being challenged. Keep an open mind and watch for cues from the interviewer.
- Think of the interviewer as a teammate and the case as a client assignment. The interview is a test of your ability to interact with your teammates and clients.
- Have fun. Interviewers are looking for people who enjoy solving problems and are fun to work with. Think of case analysis as an opportunity to discuss novel ideas and address challenging problems with smart people.

Remember that the best way to ensure that all of the above issues come to you naturally during the interview is to practice. Practice solving different cases to become more comfortable with the process.

Appendix E: Visual Reasoning Tools for Case Analysis

Using visual tools in case analysis can be extremely beneficial in illustrating your thought process and helping the interviewer understand your logic. Among the most commonly used visual reasoning tools in case analysis are flowcharts, matrixes, decision tree analysis, fishbone diagrams, estimation analysis, pie charts, and perceptual maps. Examples of each of these tools are given below.

Flowchart

A flowchart is a graphical representation of the main steps in a process. In case analysis, flowcharts can be drawn to illustrate the structure of your approach to case analysis (e.g., Goal-Strategy-Tactics-Implementation-Control), to represent the company's operations (e.g., inputs-processes-outputs), to explain the channel structure (e.g., manufacturer-retailer-consumer), etc. The benefit of using flowcharts is that they visualize and add structure to business processes, thus making them easier to explain and understand.

Matrix

	Current market	New market
Current products	Market penetration	Market development
New products	Product development	Diversification

Matrixes are a common tool for organizing qualitative data given by two (or sometimes three) variables. Matrixes are particularly useful in cases where the outcome of one of the variables is a function of the value of the other variable. The simplest and most popular form of a matrix is in the 2 x 2 matrix comprised of two variables, each with two levels. To illustrate, consider the 2 x 2 product-market matrix (also known as the Ansoff matrix). The two key variables are the product strategy and the market strategy, each with two levels: current and new. In this context, growing share by using current products depends on the market such that targeting current markets yields a market penetration strategy, whereas targeting new markets yields a market development strategy. Similarly, launching new products in current markets yields a product development strategy, whereas launching new products in new markets yields a diversification strategy.

Decision Tree Analysis

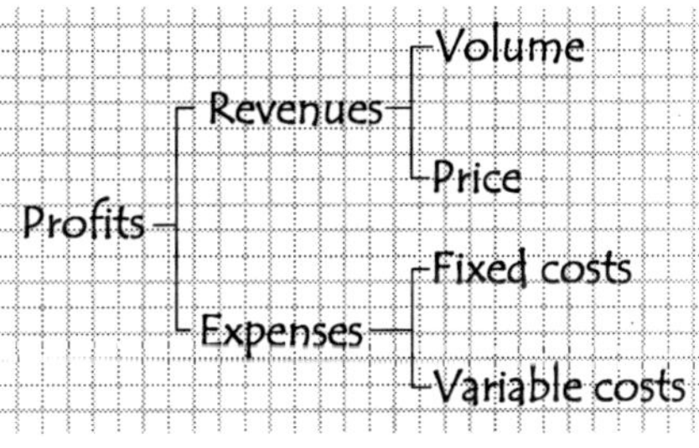

Decision tree analysis is a method of representing alternative sequential decisions and the possible outcomes from these decisions. To illustrate, a company's profits can be represented as a function of revenues and expenses, such that profits can be increased either by increasing revenues or by decreasing expenses. Increasing revenues, in turn, can be achieved either by increasing volume or by increasing the price, whereas decreasing expenses can be achieved by either lowering variable or fixed costs.

Fishbone Diagram

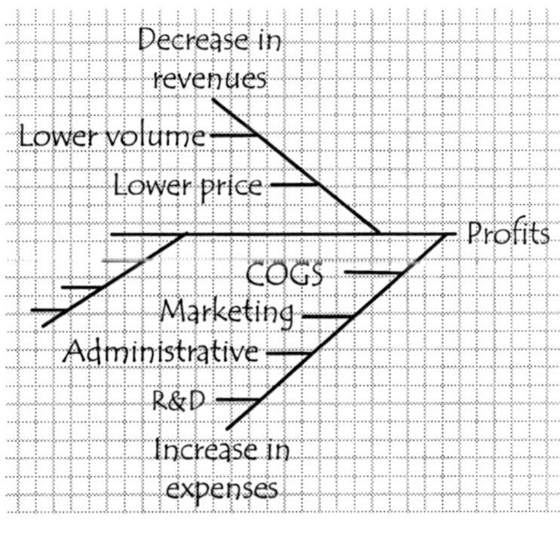

The fishbone diagram (also referred to as cause-and-effect diagram) is a graphical method commonly used for finding the most likely causes of an undesired effect. This method is also referred to as an Ishikawa diagram because it was most prominently described by the pioneer of the quality management process, Kaoru Ishikawa[1], in the 1960s. Using the fishbone diagram is very intuitive. First identify the effect you are trying to analyze and draw the "spine" of the fishbone. Next, brainstorm about the key categories of causes that could lead to the observed effect. These are the "bones" or diagonal lines starting from the "spine" and moving outward. In most cases, you should have anywhere from two to seven of these; if you have more than that, combine some of them into more general factors.[2] Finally, for each of the main causes, identify some of the most likely causes (e.g., a "cause of the cause"). These are the horizontal lines coming out of each of the bones.

Estimation Flowchart

130M All target customers → 75% → 97.5M Aware of the product → 80% → 78M Tried the product at least once → 15% → 11.7M Repeat customers

An estimation flowchart is used to illustrate the logic of quantitative analyses. To illustrate, consider the process of new service adoption. Of the 130M target customers, 75% are aware of the service; of this group, 80% have tried the product at least once, but only 15% of those who tried the product became repeat customers. An estimation flowchart can be used to illustrate that the key priority for the company is increasing the retention rate; increasing the advertising and/or offering incentives to try the product are not a major problem for the company.

Pie Chart

Pie charts are used as a visual representation of information showing parts as a proportion of the whole. Pie charts are commonly used to illustrate market share and/or share growth strategies. For example, pie charts can be used to illustrate the difference between the two core market growth strategies: stealing share from the competition (share growth strategy) and growing the overall demand for the product (market growth strategy).

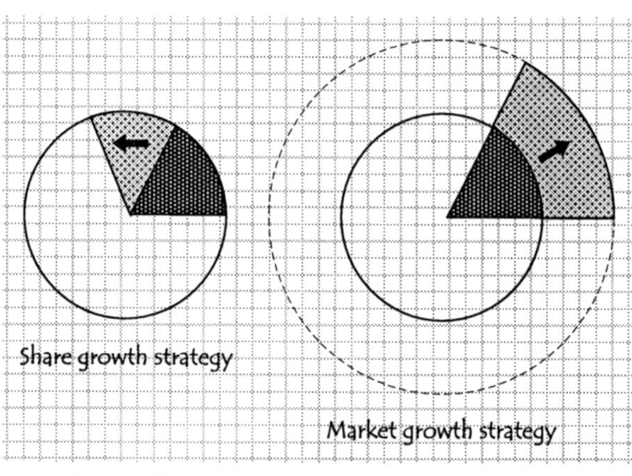

Perceptual Map

A perceptual map offers a spatial representation of the perceived relationships among objects (products, services, companies) in a set. Perceptual maps typically represent objects in a two-dimensional space defined by two variables (e.g., price and quality). Note that perceptual maps represent consumers' perception of the objects rather than the objects' actual characteristics. To illustrate, Product B in reality might be of the same quality as Product C, and yet it will be portrayed as a low-quality product if that is how it is being perceived by target customers.

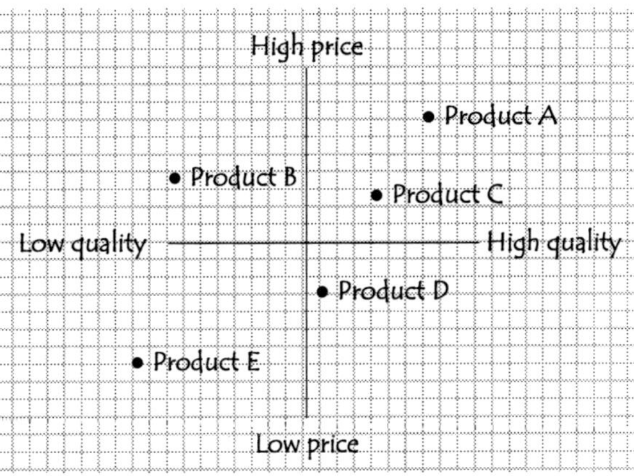

Notes

[1] Ishikawa, Kaoru (1985), *What Is Total Quality Control? The Japanese Way.* Englewood Cliffs N J: Prentice-Hall.

[2] According to Ishikawa, there are four categories of causes (the "bones") that are common to many effects: materials, machines, manpower, and methods (in case of manufacturing) and equipment, policies, procedures, and people (in case of services).

Chapter 2: The Marketing Value Framework

2.1. Introduction

Most management and strategic consulting case analyses involve a problem that is either directly or indirectly related to marketing. The concept of marketing is used in this book in a broader sense, as it was defined by the management guru Peter Drucker, who wrote:

"There is only one valid definition of business purpose: to create a customer. Because it is its purpose to create a customer, any business enterprise has two – and only these two – basic functions: marketing and innovation. Marketing is the unique, central function of the business enterprise."[1]

Because marketing plays a pivotal role in solving many of the typical management consulting and strategic management problems, understanding case analysis can greatly benefit from an initial introduction of an integrated framework for marketing analysis

The marketing value framework presented in this chapter reflects the process by which a company plans its business activities. Central to this framework is the notion that the company's ultimate success in the marketplace is determined by the soundness of the five key components of its business model as illustrated in Figure 2.1: goal, strategy, tactics, implementation, and control.

Figure 2.1. The G-S-T-I-C Framework

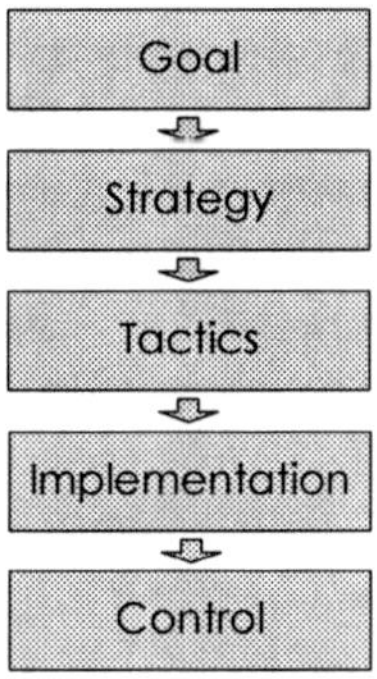

Goal
↓
Strategy
↓
Tactics
↓
Implementation
↓
Control

Because the G-S-T-I-C framework describes a generic method for making business decisions, it is used as an overarching framework to incorporate other, more specific frameworks. The different types of analysis implied by the G-S-T-I-C framework are discussed in more detail in the following sections.

2.2. Goal Analysis

In Lewis Carroll's Alice in Wonderland, when Alice asks the Cheshire Cat which path to take, he responds, "If you don't care where you're going, it doesn't make a difference which path you take." This is also very true in marketing. Without a goal, an organization can neither design an effective marketing strategy nor evaluate the success of its current strategy. Every action that a company undertakes should be consistent with a well-defined goal, thus bringing the company closer to achieving this goal.

Setting a goal typically involves two decisions: (1) identifying the focus of the company's actions and (2) the specific performance benchmarks to be reached. Setting the focus of the goal involves identifying the ultimate criterion for success, which involves factors such as profitability, revenues, and market share. In contrast, the benchmark aspect of the goal provides measurable criteria for success (e.g., increasing market share by 15%), as well as an identifiable timeframe for achieving these criteria (e.g., by the end of the fiscal year). For example, a goal might involve increasing net income (focus) by six percent by the end of the fiscal year (quantitative and temporal benchmarks). These different aspects of goals analysis are discussed in more detail below.

2.2.1. Goal Focus

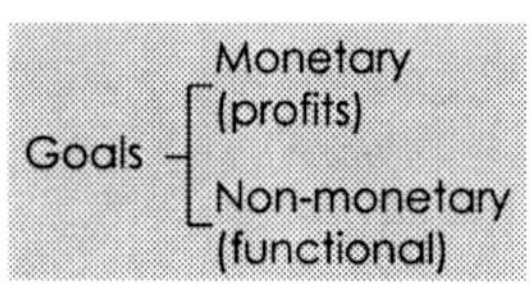

Goal analysis offers a systematic approach to understanding the sources of company value. Based on the nature of the ultimate criterion for success, two types of goals can be distinguished: (1) *monetary goals,* which are directly related to monetary factors such as increasing the company's profits, and (2) *non-monetary goals,* which are not directly linked to monetary factors and do not directly contribute to the company's bottom line. These two types of goals are discussed in more detail below.

▸ *Non-Monetary Goals*

Non-monetary goals, also referred to as functional goals, are not directly related to profitability. To illustrate, a company's strategic actions can also be guided by the desire to increase customer welfare. Thus, in the case of non-profit companies, customer welfare is the key strategic goal and profitability is set at zero, making it more of a constraint than a goal. Even companies whose primary goal is to maximize profits often have specific offerings that are not designed to directly influence the company's bottom line and, instead, have a different function. For example, an offering's primary goal can be to facilitate other, more profitable and/or more strategically important offerings (i.e., synergy goals). To illustrate, a car manufacturer might introduce an entry-level car, not because it has immediate profit potential but to gain share among younger customers so that they are more likely to upgrade to the company's more profitable models as they become older. Another example of non-monetary goals involves strengthening or repositioning the company's image. To illustrate, Ford introduced its Escape Hybrid SUV, clearly understanding that it will never recoup its costs on the first-generation vehicle. Instead, the goals were to strengthen the company's environmentally-friendly image as well as to develop engineering expertise for future generations of hybrid vehicles.[2]

▶ *Monetary Goals*

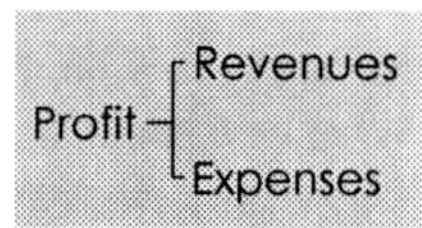

Monetary goals, such as profitability, are arguably the prevalent goals in for-profit organizations. Because profits are a function of revenues and costs, increasing profits can be achieved by decreasing expenses and/or increasing revenues. These two profit strategies are discussed in more detail below.

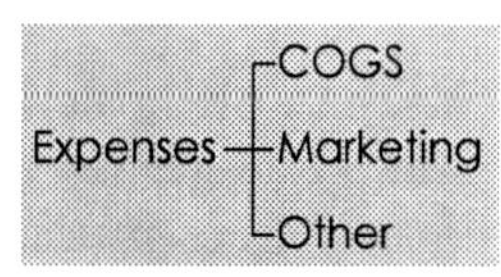

Increasing profits by lowering expenses can be achieved by decreasing one or more of the three basic types of expenses: costs of goods sold (COGS), marketing costs, and other costs, such as the cost of capital, and general and administrative costs. Most of these expenses can be further classified into two basic types: fixed costs and variable costs. Fixed costs are expenses that do not fluctuate with output volume within a relevant time period. In contrast, variable costs are expenses that fluctuate in direct proportion to the output volume of units produced. To illustrate, communication-related expenses (e.g., advertising) typically do not depend on the number of units sold and, therefore, are likely to be considered fixed marketing costs, whereas expenses incurred by consumer incentives (e.g., coupons, price discounts, and rebates) are commonly viewed as variable marketing costs. Other expenses such as channel incentives (e.g., promotional allowances) and sales force compensation can be classified either as fixed or variable costs depending on their structure (e.g., fixed salary vs. performance-based compensation).

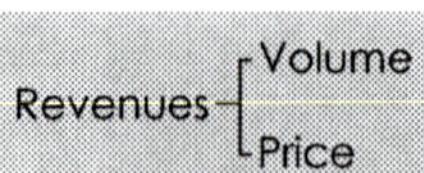

Increasing profits by increasing sales revenue can be achieved by employing two alternative strategies. Because they are a function of the number of items sold and the unit selling price, revenues can grow by either increasing the number of units sold and/or by increasing the unit selling price. Because an increase in selling price often leads to a decrease in volume, companies tend to focus on growing revenues by increasing sales volume rather than raising price. In general, there are two key aspects in designing a volume-growth strategy: defining the market strategy and defining the customer strategy. These two aspects are discussed in more detail below.

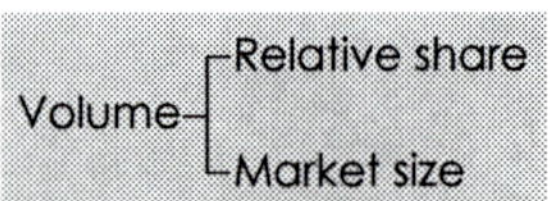

Increasing sales volume can be achieved either by stealing share from comparable offerings or by growing the overall market. The goal of the steal-share strategy is to grow the company's share by attracting customers who are already using comparable offerings. In the above example, the steal-share strategy implies promoting the company's offering in a way that encourages competitors' customers to switch.[3] In contrast, the market-growth strategy implies a focus on growing the category by bringing new customers to the market. To illustrate, promoting the benefits of high-definition television (HDTV) is likely to bring new users to the category – a strategy that will ultimately increase the number of customers switching to HDTV and benefit all companies in the HDTV market.

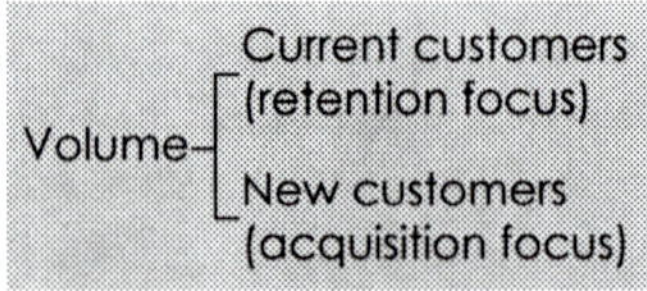

In addition to deciding on the source of volume from the market standpoint (stealing share vs. growing the overall category demand), companies can achieve sales growth either by focusing on increasing sales to current customers or by attracting new customers. Note that in contrast to growing overall market demand, where the term "new customers" refers to customers that are new to the category, the term "new customers" in the context of increasing market share refers to customers who are new to the company, regardless of whether they are new to the category. In this context, the focus on increasing sales to current customers can be linked to the company's efforts to retain its current customers; whereas, the focus on growing volume by increasing sales to new customers often reflects the company's efforts to acquire new customers.

Based on their level of specificity, a company's goals can be structured in the form of a hierarchical decision tree which outlines the relationship between different types of goals. A hierarchical map of different decision goals is illustrated in Figure 2.2.

Figure 2.2. Hierarchical Goal Map

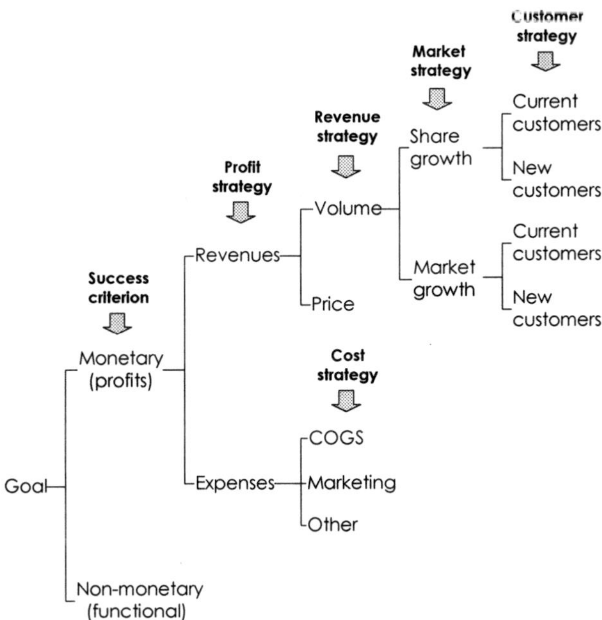

2.2.2. Performance Benchmarks

In addition to determining its focus, setting an offering's strategic goal also involves identifying the performance benchmark(s) that will be used to evaluate the success of the marketing program. Two types of benchmarks can be distinguished: quantitative and temporal.

As implied by their name, *quantitative benchmarks* define the specific milestones to be achieved by the company with respect to their focal goals. For example, benchmarks such as "increase market share by 2%," "increase retention rates by 12%," and "improve the effectiveness of the marketing expenditures by 15%" quantify the selected goal.

Setting a *timeline* for achieving a given set of goals is a key strategic decision because the strategy adopted to implement these goals is often contingent on the time horizon. To illustrate, the goal of maximizing the next-quarter profitability will likely require different strategy and tactics than the goal of maximizing the longer term profitability. In fact, the time horizon for achieving an offering's goals is often a source of potential conflicts among the company's stakeholders. To illustrate, short-term investors and many analysts tend to focus on the short-term performance reflected in a company's quarterly results, whereas longer term investors tend to focus on the long-term prospects of the company reflected in a company's strategic plan.

After the different aspects of the goal have been identified, the next step is to analyze the strategy that the organization will follow in order to achieve its goal.

2.3. Strategy Analysis

Strategy analysis outlines the logic of the company's actions aimed at achieving its goals. Strategy analysis involves two key components: (1) understanding market structure and (2) optimizing the value exchange. Market structure analysis involves identifying the key market players, such as target customers, the company, and its collaborators and competitors, as well as the overall environment in which the company operates. Value analysis, on the other hand, involves optimizing the value proposition of the company's offering to the relevant market participants: customers, the company, and its collaborators. These two components of marketing analysis are discussed in more detail below.

2.3.1. Understanding Market Structure: The 5-C Framework

The goal of market structure analysis is to identify the key market players as well as the context that serves as the background for the marketing exchange. Market structure analysis involves evaluating the following five factors, often referred to as the

"Five Cs": (1) customers, (2) the company, (3) collaborators working with the company to deliver the offering to customers, (4) competitors with offerings that provide similar benefits to the same customers, and (5) context (e.g., political, economic, social, legal, and technological) in which the company delivers its offering to customers. These five factors, visualized in Figure 2.3, are discussed in more detail below.

Figure 2.3. The 5-C Framework for Market Structure Analysis

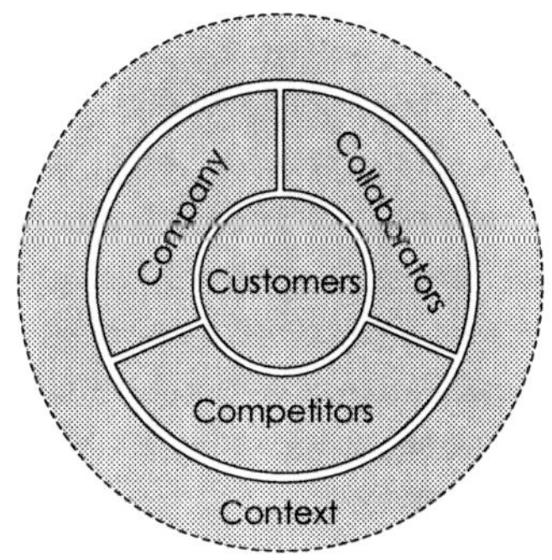

▶ *Customer Analysis*

Customer analysis aims to identify the customers for whom the offering can deliver superior value in a way that allows the company and its collaborators to achieve their strategic goals. Identifying target customers involves two aspects: identifying the *value* these customers seek from the company's offering and identifying actionable strategies to *reach* these customers. Identifying customer value involves several aspects: identifying the functional value associated with factors such as customer preferences for quality, performance, reliability, and safety; identifying the monetary value associated with factors such as willingness to pay, financing preferences, and promotion preferences; and identifying the psychological value associated with factors such as image and social status. Identifying customer reach strategies involves isolating actionable demographic, geographic, and psychographic customer characteristics that will allow the company to communicate and deliver its offering to these customers in an effective and cost-efficient manner.

▶ *Company Analysis*

Company analysis involves identifying the capabilities that enable the company to achieve its strategic goals. The cornerstone of company analysis is evaluating its strategic assets and core competencies.

Strategic assets are the company's resources that are essential for the success of the business in which the company operates and at the same time serve to differentiate the company from its competitors. From a marketing standpoint, a company's assets could include some or all of the following factors: business infrastructure (e.g., manufacturing, service, supply-chain, and management infrastructure), collaborator networks (e.g., suppliers, distributors, and collaborators in the area of technology, product development, and/or manufacturing), human capital (e.g., technological expertise, operational expertise, business expertise, customer expertise), intellectual property (e.g., patents, trademarks, copyrights), strong brands, loyal customer base, synergistic offerings, access to scarce resources, and access to capital.

Core competencies are a result of focused utilization of strategic assets and reflect the distinct areas of expertise that are critical to achieving a sustainable competitive advantage.[4]

▶ *Collaborator Analysis*

Collaborator analysis involves identifying business entities that work with the company to deliver the offering to target customers. In this context, collaboration might involve any of the following areas: product, service, brand, price, incentives, communications, and distribution. To illustrate, companies can collaborate to develop a product (research-and-development collaboration); to deliver the offering to the customer (channel collaboration); and/or to create a customer incentive (promotional collaboration).

In addition to cases of direct collaboration, companies can have complementary offerings without collaborating directly with one another. To illustrate, Belkin manufactures accessories for Apple's iPod without directly collaborating with Apple. These indirect collaborators are often referred to as complementors.

▶ *Competitive Analysis*

Competitive analysis involves identifying business entities with offerings positioned to deliver value to the same customers.

Because competitors are defined relative to the needs of the target segment, the competition often goes beyond industry-defined product categories. To illustrate, Coca-Cola competes not only with other cola producers, such as Pepsi, but also with producers of all products that could potentially fulfill the same need: juice, bottled water, and even milk. In this context, juice, bottled water, and milk are not just substitute products but rather cross-category competitors because they compete to satisfy the same need of the same target customers.

▶ *Context Analysis*

Context analysis involves evaluating factors that describe the relevant aspects of the environment in which the company delivers its offering to customers. Typical context factors include the economic, legal/regulatory, political, social, technological, and physical environment in which the marketing exchange takes place. To illustrate, the success of the Segway Human Transporter is a function of local regulations dealing with the use of powered conveyances on sidewalks and in pedestrian areas. The demand for hands-free devices is affected by the legislation requiring hands-free mobile phone use while driving in many cities. The demand for a cold medicine is likely to be affected by the flu season, and ice cream consumption is likely to be affected by the weather.

2.3.2. Value Analysis: The Marketing Value Framework

Value analysis is a process of optimizing the value associated with an offering from the viewpoint of the relevant market participants. In this context, value analysis aims to ensure that the offering can deliver superior value to target customers relative to the competition and in a way that enables the company and its collaborators to achieve their strategic goals. Therefore, an offering's value proposition should be evaluated in three different contexts: the customer's viewpoint, the company's viewpoint, and the collaborators' viewpoint.

Value analysis can be visually represented as a Venn diagram as shown in Figure 2.4. Here, the optimal value proposition is given by the overlap of the three types of value: value to the customer, value to the company, and value to collaborators. The goal of marketing analysis is, therefore, to identify the optimal value proposition – the one that maximizes the value of the offering to customers, the company, and its collaborators.

Figure 2.4. The Marketing Value Framework

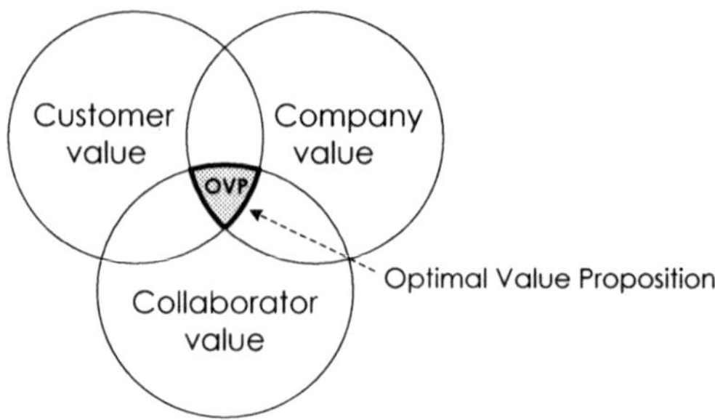

A more detailed analysis of an offering's value to customers, the company, and its collaborators involves evaluating benefits and costs associated with this offering on three dimensions: functional, monetary, and psychological (Figure 2.5). Here, functional factors refer to the benefits and costs that are directly related to an offering's performance. For example, performance (e.g., engine power), aesthetics (e.g., visual appearance), and safety (e.g., crash test performance) attributes of a car comprise this offering's functional value. Monetary factors are related to the monetary benefits and costs associated with the offering. For example, an offering's price, coupons, rebates, and cash-back offers, comprise the monetary aspect of this offering's value. Finally, psychological factors are the intangible benefits and costs associated with the offering's image. To illustrate, an offering's brand is one of the key factors comprising the psychological aspect of this offering's value.

Figure 2.5. The Three Aspects of Value Analysis

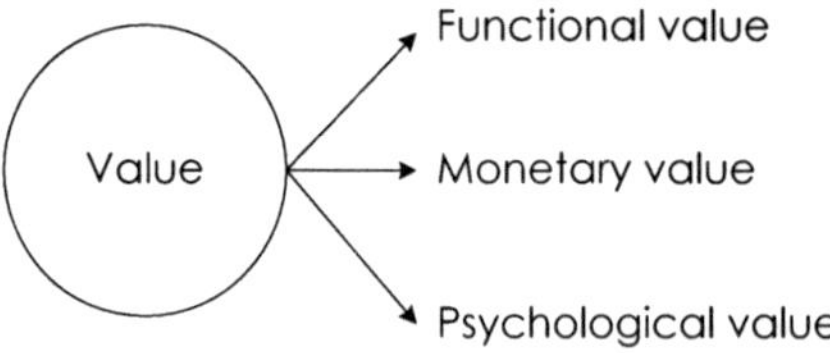

An offering's value proposition is typically reflected in this offering's *positioning*. The positioning concept reflects the company's view of how the offering should be perceived and remembered by the customer; it is the process of creating a distinct image of the company's offering in a customer's mind.[5,6] For example, BMW promotes its cars as being the "ultimate driving machine," Gillette razors aspire to be "the best a man can get," and Maytag's lonely repairman symbolizes reliability. Unlike the value proposition, which captures *all* benefits and costs associated with a particular offering, an offering's positioning reflects only the *most important aspect(s)* of its value proposition. In this context, positioning strives to present the advantages of the offering in a way that accentuates its key benefit(s) and provides customers with a compelling reason to choose and/or use the company's offering.

Because positioning involves prioritizing the existing benefits and costs of a given offering in order to highlight its key distinctive benefits, the same offering can often be positioned in multiple ways. Consider TiVo, the personal digital recorder. It offers multiple benefits such as skipping commercials, pausing live TV, one-step recording, season pass, instant replay and fast-forward features, dual-channel recording, updated program guide, etc. All of these benefits comprise TiVo's value proposition. A successful positioning requires further laddering of these benefits and identifying the single most important benefit that delivers value to the customer and differentiates TiVo from the competition. For example, TiVo could be positioned as a device that allows viewers to pause live TV (e.g., in case of a phone call), as a one-step TV recording device, or as a device that allows viewers to record one channel while watching another. In this context, positioning may require ignoring some of the offering's potential benefits to bring its distinct value advantage into focus.

2.4. Tactical Analysis

Tactical analysis identifies how the desired strategy is implemented through a set of specific marketing actions. The key marketing actions comprising an offering's value-management process and the key aspects of managing the customer, company, and collaborator value of an offering are discussed in more detail below.

2.4.1. The Value Management Process

Tactical analysis typically involves three key aspects of the value management process: creating value, communicating value, and delivering value. Value creation captures the attributes and processes that define the value of the offering to customers, the company, and its collaborators. Value communication encompasses the attributes and processes that create awareness of the offering among target customers, within the company, and to collaborators.

Finally, value delivery involves transfer of the offering value to customers, the company, and its collaborators.

Creating, communicating, and delivering value is implemented through a set of specific marketing activities commonly referred to as the marketing mix. More specifically, seven key marketing mix variables can be identified: product, service, brand, price, incentives, communication, and distribution. These seven marketing mix variables can be related to the three aspects of the value management process, as shown in Figure 2.6. Here, the product, service, brand, price and incentives comprise the value-creation aspect of the offering; communications capture the value-communication aspect; and distribution reflects the value-delivery aspect of the value management process.

Figure 2.6. The Marketing Mix

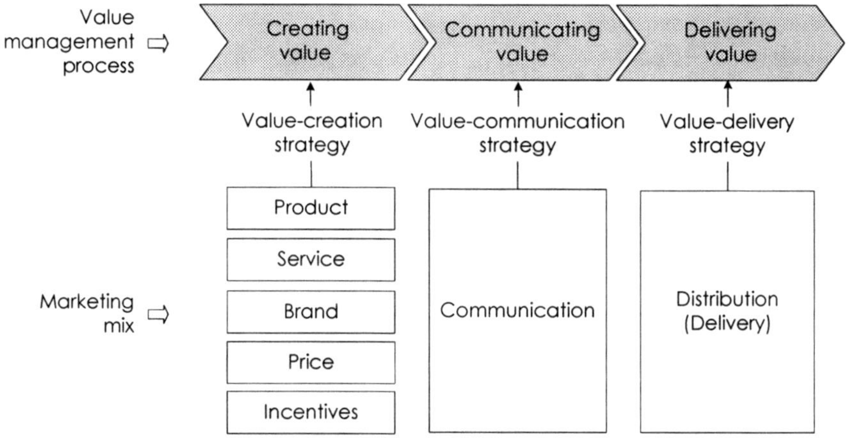

The three aspects of the value-management process – value-creation, value-communication, and value-delivery – are summarized below.

▸ *Creating Value*

The value-creation process is typically carried out through a combination of five marketing mix variables: product, service, brand, price, and incentives. The key aspects of these marketing mix variables are outlined in more detail below.

- The *product* and *service* components of the marketing mix reflect the functional characteristics of the offering. The key differences between the product and service aspect of an offering concern the change of ownership and separability. Thus, unlike products that typically change ownership in the process of the marketing exchange, services do not necessarily imply a change in ownership. In addition, unlike products that could be physically and/or temporally separated from the manufacturer, services are typically delivered and consumed at the same time, which implies that they typically cannot be inventoried or distributed through multiple distribution channels.

- The *brand* component of the marketing mix captures the characteristics of the offering typically associated with its identity and is usually the main source of the offering's psychological value. In this context, the key functions of the brand are to identify a company and/or a company's offering, to differentiate it from the competition, and to create value for customers, the company, and its collaborators. Commonly used brand elements include brand name, logo, symbol, character, and slogan.
- The *price* reflects the monetary aspect of the benefits delivered by the offering. Commonly used benchmarks for price setting are: company factors (e.g., company goals, cost structure), collaborator factors (e.g., collaborator goals, cost structure), competitive prices, and customer demand function (i.e., customers' willingness to pay). An optimal pricing strategy will typically take into account all four factors to set the optimal value to customers, the company, and its collaborators.
- *Incentives* enhance the value of the offering by providing additional benefits and/or reducing its costs. These are typically short-term solutions aimed at increasing the sales volume of the offering. Monetary incentives typically include activities such as trade allowances, volume discounts, price reductions, coupons, and rebates. Non-monetary incentives include samples, premiums, and rewards. As in the case of the other marketing mix variables, incentives need to be optimized with respect to their value to customers, the company, and its collaborators.

These five aspects of the value-creation process can be related to the three aspects of value analysis: functional value, monetary value, and psychological value (Figure 2.7). In particular, the product and service aspects of the offering contribute primarily to the functional value of the offering, the brand aspect contributes primarily to the psychological value, and the price primarily contributes to the monetary value. Note, however, that each of the five marketing mix variables could potentially contribute to all three value aspects. To illustrate, incentives could influence the functional value of the offering (especially in the case of non-monetary incentives), the monetary value of the offering (especially in the case of monetary incentives), as well as the psychological value of the offering (the psychological effect from the presence of an incentive).

Figure 2.7. Creating Value through the Marketing Mix

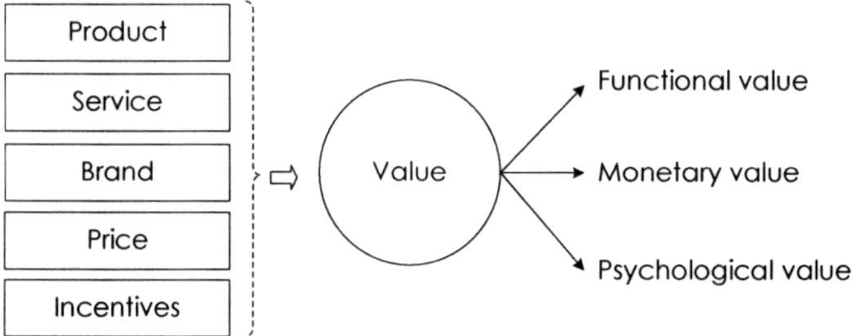

▸ *Communicating value*

The communications component of the marketing mix aims to promote the offering by informing target customers about the offering as a whole or highlighting its particular characteristics: product, service, brand, price, and incentives. The most popular means of communication is advertising in all of its forms (e.g., television, radio, print, online, outdoor, point-of-purchase, event sponsorship, and product placement). Other forms of communication include public relations aimed at generating publicity about the offering and personal selling.

▸ *Delivering value*

The distribution component of the marketing mix captures the channel structure through which the offering is delivered to the end-user. The different aspects of the value delivery include delivery of the product, service, brand, price, and incentives components of the offering. The value-delivery channels can be classified into three basic types: direct channels, in which the company delivers its offering directly to customers without relying on intermediaries; indirect channels, which typically involve one or more intermediaries (e.g., distributors, wholesalers, and/or retailers); and hybrid channels, which involve a combination of direct and indirect channels.

2.4.2. Tactical Aspects of Managing Customer, Company, and Collaborator Value

The tactical aspect of value management aims to identify and optimize the marketing mix elements, creating value for the customers, the company, and its collaborators. These three aspects of the value management process are outlined in more detail below.

▸ *Managing Customer Value*

Customer value management aims to optimize the value received by customers in the marketing exchange. Because the offering is created and delivered to customers by the company jointly with its collaborators, customer value analysis needs to account not only for the value delivered to the customer by the company but also the value customers could potentially receive from the company's collaborators. In this context, the tactical elements aimed to create customer value involve the marketing mix elements used to create, communicate, and deliver value to target customers. This involves the value delivered by the product, service, brand, price, incentives, communications, and distribution aspects of the offering.

To illustrate the customer aspect of the value-management process, consider iPod, the digital music player from Apple. From a customer's perspective, the product aspect of the iPod is the functionality offered by the digital player, such as hard-drive capacity, display, and battery life. The service aspect of the offering involves the service and technical support that come with the product, as well as the augmented services such as iTunes. The brand aspect is defined by the Apple and iPod brands, which differentiate this offering from other functionally similar offerings by iRiver, Dell, and Sony. The iPod retail price ranges from $299 to $399 depending on the configuration. Incentives include customer promotions such as rebates, educational discounts, and free music/video downloads. The communications aspect involves various forms of advertising, public relations, and product placement in newscasts, movies, and talk shows. Finally, the distribution component encompasses the channels used to deliver the offering to end-users such as Apple's online store, Apple's brick-and-mortar retail stores, and other retailers such as Best Buy and Circuit City.

▶ *Managing Collaborator Value*

Collaborator value management aims to optimize the value delivered by a particular offering to the company's collaborators. Because the collaborators work with the company to deliver the offering to target customers, collaborator value analysis needs to account not only for the value delivered to the collaborators by the company but also the value collaborators receive from the offering's customers. In this context, the tactical elements aimed to create collaborator value involve the marketing mix elements used to create, communicate, and deliver value to collaborators. This involves the value delivered by the product, service, brand, price, incentives, communications, and distribution aspects of the offering.

To illustrate the collaborator's aspect of the value-management process, consider the value of iPod to retailers such as Best Buy, Circuit City, and Amazon.com. The service aspect of the offering involves the support provided by Apple to facilitate sales and post-sales services. The brand aspect is defined by the incremental value that an association with the Apple and iPod brands brings to retailers. The price aspect reflects the difference in the iPod's wholesale and retail price. The value of incentives is a function of the incentives received by collaborators from the company and the incentives offered by collaborators to customers. The value of collaborator communications involves activities such as advertising in trade publications, sending press releases, participating in trade shows, and event sponsorship; this includes activities originating in the company and directed to its collaborators, as well as communications by collaborators aimed at the offering's target customers. Finally, the distribution aspect of the offering encompasses the channels used to deliver the offering from the company to retailers, as well as channels used to deliver the offering from retailers to the end customers.

▶ *Managing Company Value*

Company value management aims to optimize the value delivered by a particular offering by customers and the company's collaborators to the company. In this context, the tactical elements aimed at creating company value involve the benefits and costs associated with the marketing mix elements used to create, communicate, and deliver value to the company.

To illustrate, the company aspect of the value-management process, consider the value of iPod to Apple. From a monetary-value perspective, the product, service, brand, incentive, communications, and distribution aspects of the marketing mix can be viewed as the costs associated with developing the iPod, whereas the benefits are reflected in the price-driven revenues received from its customers and collaborators. From the functional perspective, the process of developing the iPod creates value for Apple by positioning the company as a product development leader in the portable music player category. The process of building the iPod brand adds to Apple's expertise in brand building. The process of establishing its own brick-and-mortar distribution outlets adds to Apple's expertise in the area of retailing. Finally, from a psychological perspective, the success of the iPod creates value for Apple by enhancing the company's image, which in turn affects Apple's ability to recruit and retain skilled employees.

2.5. Implementation and Control

The implementation component of market planning outlines the timeline and the algorithm of executing the offering's strategy and tactics. It also identifies contingency strategies for alternative actions, depending on changes in the marketing environment. The implementation aspect of marketing analysis involves two key factors: the processes that enable the company to implement its strategy and the people managing these processes.

The *processes* underlying an offering are the logistics that enable the company to achieve its goal and, at the same time, deliver value to its customers and collaborators. Processes can include product development practices, service delivery infrastructure, brand-building mechanisms, and distribution channel structure. To illustrate, consider the process of launching a new service with certain characteristics, such as hours of operation, refund policy, and level of service support. In this context, implementation involves processes such as managerial infrastructure, trained customer service representatives, and customer management policies, which underlie the service aspect of the value-creation, value-communication, and value-delivery processes.

People are the other key aspect of implementing a particular marketing strategy. The human-resource aspect of implementation involves the core skills and knowledge of the people involved in creating, communicating, and delivering value. The core personnel skills include leadership, analytical skills, creativity, teamwork, communication skills, management skills, capacity to learn, and drive. The knowledge factor includes employees' functional knowledge (e.g., marketing, accounting, or finance), industry knowledge (e.g., wireless communications, plastics, or nanotechnology), and global knowledge (e.g., country-specific or region-specific).

To ensure successful implementation of its strategy and tactics, a company needs to track results and monitor changes in the environment in which it operates. Implementing a system for tracking results is vital to a company's success in the market because it ensures consistency between the desired performance benchmarks and the company's actual performance. Without a system in place to account for the results of its actions, a company has no knowledge of the effectiveness and the efficiency of its strategy and tactics.

Having a control system allows the company to monitor the changes in the marketplace in which the company operates, such as changes in the characteristics of the target customers (e.g., preferences, price sensitivity, demographics, etc.), changes in the collaborative environment (e.g., power, consolidation, profit margins, etc.), and changes in the competitive landscape (number, size, and goals of competitors, nature of the competition, etc.), as well as changes in different aspects of the business environment in general (e.g. legal, political, social, economic, and technological).

In general, controls could be applied to each of the four stages of marketing analysis: goal, strategy, tactics, and implementation. Thus, controls involve (1) evaluating the viability of the company's goals, (2) monitoring the changes in the market structure and the processes involved in optimizing the value of the offering to customers, the company, and its collaborators, (3) evaluating the processes of creating, communicating, and delivering value, and finally (4) monitoring the effectiveness of translating the planned strategy and tactics into action (Figure 2.8).

Figure 2.8. Market Planning and Control

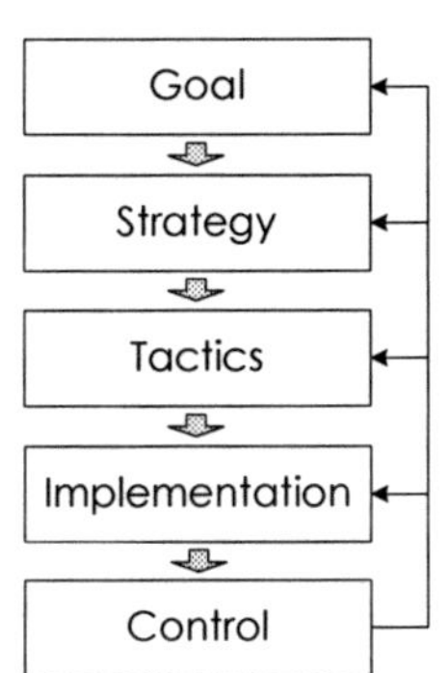

2.6. The Big Picture

To summarize, the framework for strategic marketing analysis advanced here comprises the following five components:

- The *goal* reflects a gap between the company's actual and potential accomplishments, between what the company readily has (in terms of profits, revenues, and/or market share) and what it could have. To illustrate, a company's goal to increase its market share is a reflection of the strategic gap between its current share and the potential to steal share from competitors.
- The *strategy* outlines the logic of the company's actions aimed at achieving its goals. Strategy analysis involves two key components: identifying market structure (i.e., identifying the key market players and the overall environment in which the company operates) and optimizing the value proposition of the company's offering to all relevant market participants.
- The *tactics* identify how the desired strategy will be implemented through a set of explicit business activities. Tactics typically involve designing a set of specific marketing mix variables (e.g., product, service, brand, price, incentives, communications, and distribution) aimed at creating, communicating, and delivering value to target customers.
- The *implementation* component of market planning identifies the key personnel and outlines the essential processes involved in executing the offering's strategy and tactics.

- The *control* aspect of market planning outlines the policy to measure progress toward the company's strategic goals, monitor performance, identify potential problems, and make adjustments when necessary.

These five aspects of strategic marketing analysis comprise the Strategic Analysis Pyramid shown in Figure 2.9.

Figure 2.9: The Strategic Analysis Pyramid

2.7. The Marketing Plan

The strategic marketing analysis process is typically formalized as a marketing plan. The process of writing a marketing plan is often used synonymously with strategic planning. Equating the writing of a marketing plan with strategic planning, however, is wrong: strategic planning and the writing of a plan are two fundamentally different activities. Strategic planning is the process of conceptualizing the company's goals and developing strategies and tactics to achieve these goals. Writing a marketing plan involves capturing on paper the outcome of the strategic planning process.

There is no unique template for writing a marketing plan; different companies recommend different approaches. At the same time, most marketing plans share the same structural elements.

The marketing plan outlined below integrates these common elements by linking them to the strategic marketing analysis framework outlined in this note. In this context, a company's marketing plan is comprised of the following six key components: executive summary, goal, strategy, tactics, implementation, and control.

The marketing plan begins with an executive summary, which offers a succinct overview of the key aspects of the proposed course of action, as well as its rationale. The executive summary is followed by an outline of the company's goals. Following the goal analysis is a description of the company's strategy, which identifies the market structure and outlines the offering's value proposition to the company, its customers, and collaborators. The strategy analysis is then followed by a description of marketing tactics capturing the processes of creating, communicating, and delivering value. Following the tactical analysis, the implementation plan outlines the processes and resources for executing the offering's strategy and tactics. The control section describes a company's policy used to measure the progress toward the company's strategic goals, monitor performance, identify potential problems, and make adjustments when necessary (Figure 2.10).

Figure 2.10: The Strategic Marketing Analysis Pyramid

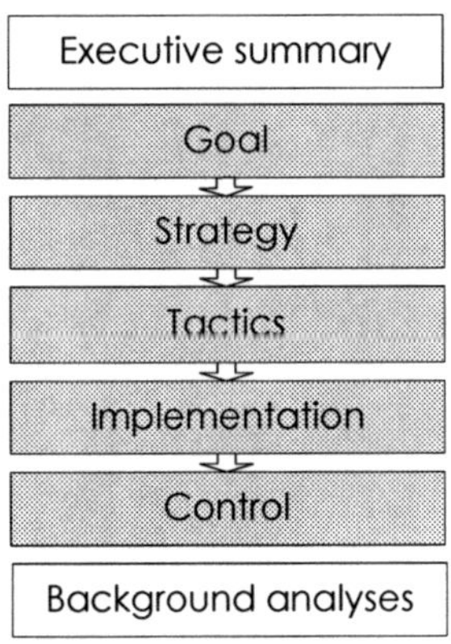

The background analyses section contains all information that is not an integral part of the company's value strategy and, instead, provides auxiliary analyses that offer more detailed understanding of particular aspects of the company's business plan. Information typically included in the background analyses might involve detailed company analysis, industry analysis, competition analysis, detailed financial calculations, profitability projections and what-if scenarios, etc. The goal of separating these background analyses into a separate section is to streamline the description of the logic of the value exchange process so that the reader can clearly see how management intends to satisfy customer needs better than the competition in a way that enables the company and its collaborators to achieve their strategic goals.

Notes

---

[1] Drucker, Peter (1954), *The Practice of Management.* New York, NY: HarperCollins.

[2] Fortune (2004), The New Escape Hybrid's a Sure Hit – But It Flunks the Profit Test, June 28

[3] Note that the steal-share strategy can also be used with respect to offerings by the same company. To illustrate, Gillette's MACH3 razor was designed to induce Sensor users to trade up, thus cannibalizing the sales of the Sensor product line.

[4] Prahalad, C. K. and Gary Hamel (1990), "The Core Competence of the Corporation," *Harvard Business Review* (May-June).

[5] Kotler, Philip (1984), *Marketing Management: Analysis, Planning, and Control* (5th ed.). Englewood Cliffs, NJ: Prentice-Hall.

[6] Ries, Al and Jack Trout (2001), *Positioning: The Battle for Your Mind* (20th anniversary ed.). New York, NY: McGraw-Hill.

Chapter 3: Case Problems and Solutions

3.1. Common Business Case Problems

Cases vary in scope: Some are more specific and concern a particular offering, whereas others are more general in scope and involve the entire company. Additionally, cases vary in terms of the nature of the underlying problem. Some cases involve planning new actions, others involve optimizing the performance of ongoing activities, and still others involve evaluating the impact of external factors on the company's performance. The various types of cases are discussed in more detail below.

Depending on their level of generality, most business cases can be classified into one of two categories: offering-focused cases and company-focused cases.

- *Offering-focused cases* deal with issues particular to a single offering. To illustrate, estimating the market potential for a new product, increasing the share of an existing product, and developing a response strategy to a competitive action exemplify typical offering-focused cases.
- *Company-focused cases* have the broadest scope and deal with issues involving multiple unrelated offerings and/or product lines within the company. To illustrate, the development of strategies for allocating resources across a company's different business units, evaluating the viability of an acquisition strategy, and developing company-wide strategies for maximizing the shareholders value exemplify common company-focused cases.

Depending on the nature of the underlying problem, most business cases can be further classified into one of three types: planning cases, performance-gap cases, and external-change cases. These three case types are discussed in more detail below.

- *Planning cases* typically involve the development of a strategic, tactical, and/or implementation plan to achieve a certain goal. Planning cases might involve the entire company, a specific product line, or an offering. To illustrate, company-specific planning cases typically involve developing a plan to achieve a certain company-wide goal, such as increasing profitability and/or increasing revenues. In contrast, product-line cases involve developing a plan to achieve a certain product-line goal such as launching multiple product line extensions, and finally, offering cases focus on developing a plan to achieve an offering-specific goal such as launching a new product or increasing share of an existing offering.

- *Performance-gap cases* are characterized by the presence of a discrepancy between the desired and the actual state of affairs, between the goal and the reality. To illustrate, a decrease in a company's profitability (the problem) can be viewed as a strategic gap between the company's desire to strengthen its market position (goal) and the decrease in market share (reality). Other examples of performance gaps include discrepancies between desired and actual net income, profit margins, and revenues. In this context, the goal of case analysis is to solve the problem by identifying its source and suggesting a viable strategy to close the performance gap.
- *External-change cases* depict scenarios that involve a significant change in the context in which the company operates. Such changes might include a new competitive entry, a competitive (re)action (e.g., new product introduction, price change, aggressive promotions, superiority claims), changes in customer demand, changes in technology, legal regulations, and government policies. In this context, the goal of case analysis is to evaluate the impact of the external change on the company's activities.

Note that planning, performance-gap, and external-change cases can vary in scope and can involve issues concerning a specific offering or the entire company. In this context, the different types of cases can be summarized in the form of a 2 x 3 matrix as shown in Figure 3.1.

Figure 3.1. Share-Growth and Market-Growth Strategies

	Offering focus	Company focus
Planning cases	Develop an offering plan	Develop a company plan
Performance-gap cases	Improve an offering's performance	Improve a company's performance
External-change cases	Evaluate the impact of an external factor on an offering's performance	Evaluate the impact of an external factor on a company's performance

3.2. Frameworks for Solving Planning Cases

As discussed in the previous section, most of the planning cases fall into one of two categories: cases concerning a particular offering and cases concerning the entire company. Some of the key frameworks for solving these different types of cases are discussed in more detail below.

3.2.1. Offering-Focused Case Frameworks

Most offering-focused action-planning cases can be solved by applying the Goal-Strategy-Tactics-Implementation-Control framework (G-S-T-I-C) outlined in the previous chapter. Central to this framework is the notion that the company's ultimate success in the marketplace is determined by the soundness of its five key components: goal, strategy, tactics, implementation, and control.

The G-S-T-I-C framework can be applied to solving several types of planning cases: those focused on developing an offering's strategy (e.g., identifying the key market factors such as target customers, collaborators, competitors, context factors, as well as developing an offering's overall value proposition); cases focused on identifying the tactical aspects of an offering (e.g., product, service, brand, price, incentives, communications, and distribution); cases focused on developing an implementation plan; and, finally, cases focused on developing a system for tracking the progress and monitoring the environment. A detailed overview of the G-S-T-I-C framework is offered in Chapter 2.

3.2.2. Company-Focused Case Frameworks

Company-focused action-planning cases deal with issues concerning the entire company rather than focusing on a specific offering. As the level of generality increases, the marketing planning also becomes increasingly complex, focusing on the interdependencies across different offerings and product lines. As a result, company-focused cases are more likely to adopt a more general, portfolio-analysis approach to evaluating the pros and cons of individual offerings relative to one another. In this context, three of the most relevant frameworks are the product-market growth framework, the SWOT framework, and the five forces framework. These three frameworks are discussed in more detail below.

▶ *The Product-Market Growth Framework*

The product-market growth framework, introduced by Igor Ansoff,[1] identifies four distinct market-growth strategies based on the type of offering (existing vs. new) and the type of customers (current vs. new). The resulting 2 x 2 matrix contains four product-market strategies commonly referred to as (1) market penetration, (2) market development, (3) product development, and (4) diversification (Figure 3.2).

Figure 3.2. Product-Market Growth Matrix[2]

	Current Customers	New Customers
Current Products	Market penetration	Market development
New Products	Product development	Diversification

Market-penetration strategies aim at increasing the sales of an existing offering to a company's current customers. A common market-penetration strategy is increasing the usage rate. To illustrate, airlines stimulate demand from current customers by adopting frequent-flyer programs; packaged goods manufacturers enclose re-purchase coupons as part of their product offerings; orange juice manufacturers promote drinking orange juice throughout the day rather than for breakfast only.

Market-development strategies aim to grow sales by introducing an existing offering to new customers. In this case, the company builds on the success of its offerings to attract new customers. The two most common market-development strategies include targeting a new customer segment in an existing geographic area and introducing the offering to a different geographic area (e.g., exporting products to a new country). Market-development strategies aimed at attracting new customers include price promotions (e.g., price reductions, coupons, and rebates), new distribution channels, and communication strategies focused on different customer segment(s).

Product-development strategies target sales growth by developing new (to the company) offerings for existing customers. In this case, the company builds on its current customer base by offering new products. The two most common market-development strategies include developing entirely new offerings (product innovation) or extending the current product line by modifying existing offerings (product line extension). In this context, product line extensions are often achieved by adding different sizes, forms, flavors, or colors, while preserving the core set of benefits of the original offering.

Diversification strategies aim at growing sales by introducing new offerings to new customers. Because both the offering and the customers are new to the company, this strategy is riskier than any of the other product-market strategies. The primary rationale for diversification is to take advantage of growth opportunities in areas in which the company has no presence.

▶ *The SWOT Framework*

The SWOT framework is a relatively simple, extremely flexible, and very intuitive approach for evaluating a company's overall business condition (SWOT stands for Strengths, Weaknesses, Opportunities, and Threats). SWOT analysis is typically used to evaluate the overall health of a particular company and is especially useful for solving cases involving company-related investments, mergers, and/or acquisitions.

The SWOT framework calls for compartmentalizing all factors describing the company, and the environment in which it operates, into four categories: strengths, weaknesses, opportunities, and threats. These factors can be viewed on two dimensions: (1) whether they are internal or external to the company, and (2) whether they are favorable or unfavorable from the company's standpoint. The resulting 2 x 2 SWOT matrix is shown in Figure 3.3.

Figure 3.3. SWOT Matrix

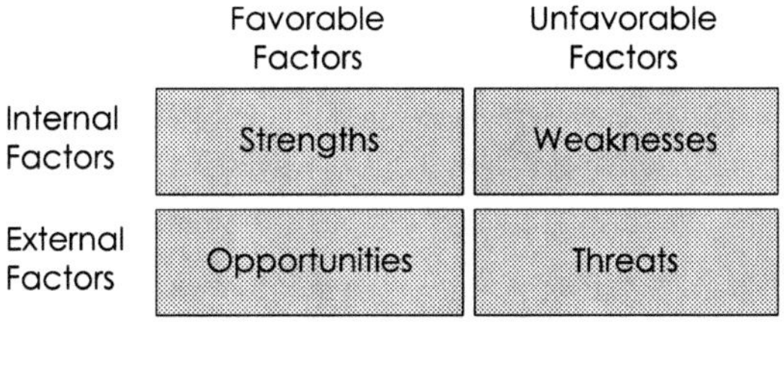

	Favorable Factors	Unfavorable Factors
Internal Factors	Strengths	Weaknesses
External Factors	Opportunities	Threats

For example, factors such as loyal customers, strong brand name(s), strategically important patents and trademarks, know-how, experienced personnel, and access to scarce resources would be classified as strengths; whereas, factors such as disloyal customers, diluted brand name, and lack of technological expertise would be classified as weaknesses. Similarly, factors such as emergence of a new, underserved customer segment, low price-sensitivity customers, and a favorable economic environment would be classified as opportunities. In contrast, issues such as a new competitive entry into the category, increased product commoditization, and increased buyer and/or supplier power would be classified as threats.

▶ *The Five Forces Framework*

The Five Forces framework was advanced by Michael Porter[3] as a conceptual approach for industry-based analysis of the nature of the competition. This framework is often used for strategic industry-level decisions such as evaluating the viability of entering (or exiting from) a particular industry.

According to the Five Forces framework, the competitiveness within an industry is determined by evaluating the following five factors: bargaining power of suppliers, bargaining power of buyers, threat of new entrants, threat of substitutes, and rivalry among extant competitors (Figure 3.4). The joint impact of these five factors determines the competitive environment in which a firm operates and allows the firm to anticipate competitors' actions. The five forces influencing the state of competition in an industry can be summarized as follows:

Figure 3.4. The Five Forces of Competition[4]

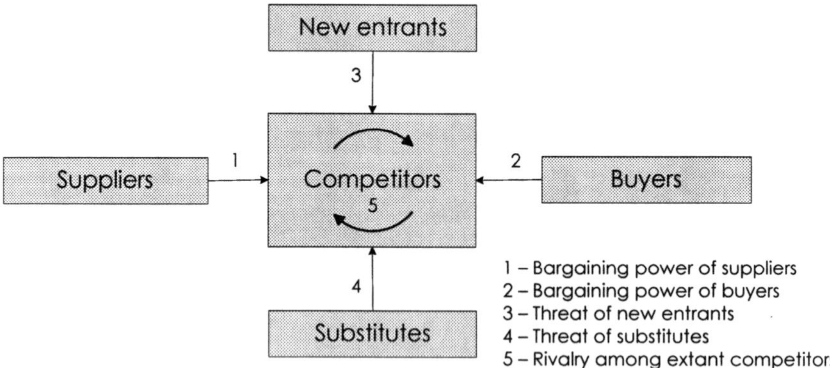

Bargaining power of suppliers – A supplier group is powerful when: it is dominated by a few companies; the product is differentiated and/or has switching costs; the product has diverse applications (e.g., across industries); the product poses a credible threat of forward integration.

Bargaining power of buyers – A buyer group is powerful when: it has concentrated, large-volume purchases; the supplied product is undifferentiated and has no switching costs; the product represents a substantial part of buyers' costs (hence encouraging more price shopping); the buyer's profit margins are low; the product is not crucial for the buyer; there is a credible threat of backward integration.

Threat of new entrants – The greater the threat, the greater the overall industry competitiveness. There are six main entry barriers:

- Economies of scale – the benefits from operating the business on a large scale (e.g., in terms of production, research, marketing, service, distribution, or utilization of the sales force and financing). As a general rule, large economies of scale tend to deter new entrants.
- Product differentiation – the degree to which competitive products are perceived by consumers to be different. In general, the presence of highly differentiated products is viewed as a deterrent for new entrants.
- Capital requirements – the magnitude of financial resources required to enter the industry. High capital requirements are likely to deter new entrants.
- Cost disadvantages (independent of size) – factors such as experience-curve effects, government subsidies, or favorable locations;
- Access to distribution channels – ability to place their offering in the desired distributors. Limited access to distribution channels tends to serve as a deterrent for new entrants;
- Government policy – regulations, license requirements, and access to technologies (e.g., airlines, power generation, and liquor).

Threat of substitute products or services – The introduction of new products tends to increase the competition in an industry and limit the profitability of an industry. In general, the threat of substitutes tends to be greater in cases when the substitutes have clear advantages over the existing products and/or when the profit margins in the industry producing the substitute product are relatively high.

Rivalry among existing competitors – In general, rivalry tends to be stronger in cases when: existing competitors are numerous and comparable in size and power (and hence are likely to have similar goals); industry growth is slow (leading to fights for redistribution of the existing market share); the product is non-differentiated (leading to price-based competition); the fixed costs are high and/or the product is perishable, there is excess capacity, the exit barriers are high; rivals are very diverse in terms of goals, strategies, and/or organizational culture.

Notes

---

[1] Ansoff, H. Igor (1979), *Strategic Management.* New York, NY: Wiley.

[2] Adapted from Ibid.

[3] Porter, Michael E. (1979), "How Competitive Forces Shape Strategy," *Harvard Business Review*, 57, 137-145.

[4] Adapted from Ibid.

3.3. General Solutions for Planning Cases

Most planning cases fall into one of two categories: cases involving a specific offering and cases involving the entire company. Depending on the nature of the underlying problem, offering-focused cases can be further organized into two types: cases concerning the strategic aspects of a particular offering and cases concerning the tactical aspects of a particular offering. General solutions for these different types of planning cases are outlined below.

3.3.1. Offering Strategy Cases

The general approach to solve offering-strategy cases is derived from the G-S-T-I-C framework; it involves three key steps: (1) identifying the underlying goal, (2) developing the strategy to achieve that goal, and (3) identifying the tactical, implementation, and control aspects of the offering (Figure 3.5). The most common strategic problem involves developing (or evaluating) a plan for launching a new offering. A general solution for cases involving a new product/service launch is given below.

Figure 3.5. Strategy Development

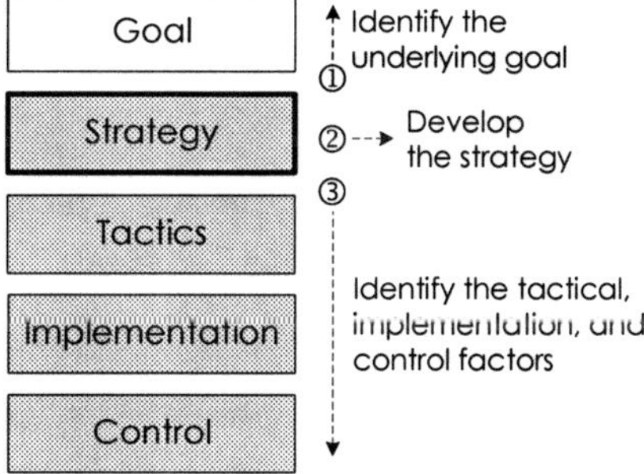

➲ *Launching a New Offering*

Example: Your client is considering launching a new product. What should you consider in bringing the product to market?

Solving new product development cases is a direct application of the framework for solving planning cases, outlined in the previous chapter. A systematic approach to developing a marketing plan for launching a new product/service is to follow the G-S-T-I-C framework. This approach involves the following three steps:

⇨ Step 1: Identify the Goal

The first step is to identify the goal that the company is trying to achieve with this offering. The key questions to ask are:

- What is the *scope* of the goal (e.g., profitability, revenues, or market share)? Is the goal for the product to have a direct monetary impact on the company's bottom line or is its primary goal to facilitate another, complementary offering?
- What are the specific *performance benchmarks* that will qualify the launch of the new product as a success?
- What is the *timeframe* to achieve the goal?

For example, an offering goal might be to increase market share (scope) by 10% (performance benchmark) within the first two years (timeframe).

⇨ Step 2: Identify the Key Market Factors and the Value of the Offering to the Relevant Market Participants

A useful approach to evaluating market structure is to follow the 5-C (customers, company, collaborations, competition, and context) and 3-V (customer value, company value, and collaborator value) frameworks introduced in the previous chapter. This approach implies the following analyses:

- **Customer analysis**
  - *Identify target customers.* The key questions to ask here are:
    - Who is (and who is not) targeted by this offering?
    - What are the underlying needs that define the target segment?
    - Are these customers new to the company or are they already using the company's other products?
    - Are these customers new to the category or are they currently using a competitor's product?
  - *Define the offering's value proposition to target customers.* The key questions to ask here are:
    - What is the customer value to be delivered by the offering?

  - What are the key benefits and costs to the customer? What makes this offering superior, relative to the other offerings in the marketplace?

- **Company analysis**
  - *Identify the company's capability to deliver value to the target customers.* The key question to ask here is:
    - What are the core competencies and strategic assets that will enable the company's offering to satisfy the needs of the target customers better than the competitive offerings?
  - *Define the offering's value to the company.* The key questions to ask here are:
    - What value is the offering delivering to the company?
    - What are the key benefits and costs to the company?
    - How does this offering help the company achieve its goals? What is the value added by this offering, given the existing offerings in the company's product line (if applicable)?
    - Does this offering have synergies with the company's other offerings?
    - Is there a threat of cannibalization and, if yes, what is the profit impact of such cannibalization?
- **Collaborator analysis (if applicable)**
  - *Identify collaborators.* The key question to ask here is:
    - What are the business entities that work with the company to deliver the offering to target customers (e.g., channel partners, marketing partners, suppliers, ingredient manufacturers, etc.)?
  - *Define the value to collaborators.* The key questions to ask here are:
    - Why would the company's collaborators support this offering?
    - How does this offering help collaborators achieve their goals?

  - What makes this offering superior from a collaborator's standpoint, relative to the other offerings by the same company and/or by the competition?

- **Competitor analysis**
  - *Identify current competitors.* The key questions to ask here are:
    - What are the key competitive offerings that deliver similar benefits to the same target customers?
    - Do companies offering these competing products/services have a sustainable competitive advantage?
  - *Identify potential and future competitors.* The key questions to ask here are:
    - What is the likelihood of new offerings entering the competitive landscape?
    - Are there substantial barriers to entry/exit?
    - Is the industry growth/profitability attractive enough to encourage new entrants?
- **Context analysis**
  - *Identify the relevant context factors.* The key questions to ask here are:
    - What context factors (e.g., economic, technological, legal/regulatory, social, and political) affect the performance of the company's offering in the marketplace?
    - How are these context factors likely to change in the future? What are the current trends?

The development of an offering's strategy is followed by designing the tactical, implementation, and control aspects of the offering.

⇨ Step 3: Design the Tactical, Implementation, and Control Aspects of the Offering

The *tactical aspect* of the offering identifies how the desired strategy will be implemented through a set of specific actions. The goal of tactical analysis is to ensure that the particular tactical solution will enable the company to implement the chosen strategy and achieve its goals. A particularly useful approach at this stage is analyzing the effectiveness of the seven marketing mix variables (product, service, brand, price, incentives, communications, and distribution). Because questions related to these marketing mix factors are often given as separate cases, general case solutions for these cases are addressed in more detail in the following section.

Designing an *implementation aspect* of the offering involves identifying the processes that underlie each of the marketing mix variables. This step calls for analyzing the logistics that enable the company to implement its strategic and tactical decisions. In particular, the implementation component of market planning outlines (1) the algorithm of executing the offering's strategy and tactics, (2) the timeline, and (3) the contingency strategies for alternative actions depending on changes in the marketing environment. In this context, implementation often involves analyzing the product development processes, service delivery infrastructure, brand building mechanisms, pricing algorithms, incentives design, communications infrastructure, and distribution channel design. To illustrate, consider a case in which a company is launching a new service and is trying to develop an optimal service management strategy. In this context, the implementation decision involves designing the processes that enable the company and its collaborators to deliver and receive value by implementing its service strategy (e.g., managerial infrastructure, training customer service representatives, and identifying customer management policies).

Finally, designing the *control aspect* of the offering involves outlining a policy to measure the progress toward the company's strategic goals, monitor performance, identify potential problems, and make adjustments when necessary.

3.3.2. Offering Tactics Cases

Similar to the offering-strategy cases, the general approach to solve offering-tactics cases is derived from the G-S-T-I-C framework and incorporates the following three key steps: (1) identifying the underlying goal and the strategy to achieve that goal, (2) planning the tactical aspects of the offering, and (3) developing the implementation and control aspects of the offering (Figure 3.6). The most common tactical problems can be derived from the 7-M framework and involve cases related to product, service, brand, price, incentives, communications, and distribution aspects of the offering. General solutions for cases involving these issues are given below.

Figure 3.6. Strategy Development

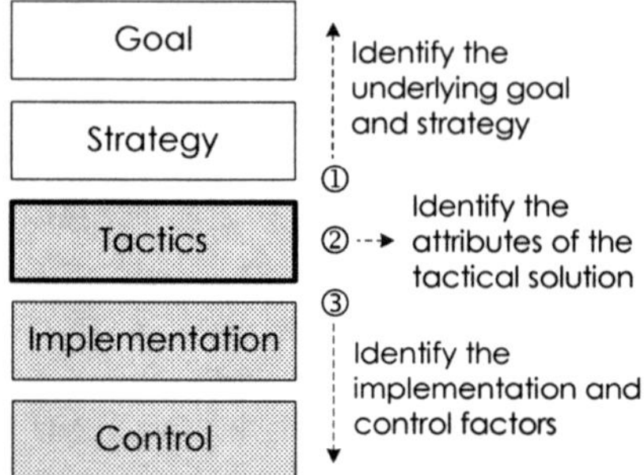

➲ *Developing a Product/Service Strategy and Tactics*

Example: The research and development team devises a new formula to revitalize your product. What questions would you ask to evaluate this improvement?

The key steps to developing a successful product/service strategy and tactics are:

⇨ **Step 1: Identify the underlying goal and strategy of the offering**

- Identify the goals to be achieved by the offering
- Identify the strategy adopted to achieve the goal (e.g., who are the target customers, what need does the offering satisfy, what other products can be used to satisfy the same need, how is the target offering different from the competitive offerings)
- Identify the characteristics of the other marketing mix variables (i.e., brand, price, incentives, communications, distribution)

⇨ **Step 2: Identify the key aspects of the product/service**

- Identify the key attributes (e.g., functionality, design, physical dimensions, hours of operation, refund policy, and level of service support) describing the product/service

- Identify how these attributes map into specific customer benefits.

⇨ **Step 3: Design the implementation and control factors**

- Develop a plan to implement the proposed solution
- Design a mechanism to monitor progress and evaluate success

➲ *Developing a Branding Strategy and Tactics*

Example: A department store in Chicago is buying an equally prestigious department store in another city and changing that store's name to match its own. How do you handle changing the name of the store?

The key steps to developing a successful branding strategy and tactics are:

⇨ **Step 1: Identify the underlying goal and strategy of the offering**

- Identify the goals to be achieved by the offering
- Identify the strategy adopted to achieve the goal (e.g., who are the target customers, what need does the offering satisfy, what other products can be used to satisfy the same need, how is the target offering different from the competitive offerings)
- Identify the characteristics of the other marketing mix variables (i.e., product, service, price, incentives, communications, distribution)

⇨ **Step 2: Identify the key aspects of the brand**

- Identify the key branding elements (e.g., brand name, logo, slogan, jingle, character, and packaging)
- Identify the value added by the brand from the standpoint of customers, the company, and its collaborators

⇨ **Step 3: Design the implementation and control factors**

- Develop a plan to implement the proposed solution

- Design a mechanism to monitor progress and evaluate success

➲ *Developing a Pricing Strategy and Tactics*

Example: Develop a pricing strategy for a large ski resort

The "optimal" price is a price that, in combination with the other marketing mix variables (product, service, brand, incentives, communications, and distribution), delivers optimal value to customers, the company, and collaborators. The key steps to developing a successful pricing strategy and tactics are:

⇨ **Step 1: Identify the underlying goal and strategy of the offering**

- Identify the goals to be achieved by the offering
- Identify the strategy adopted to achieve the goal (e.g., who are the target customers, what need does the offering satisfy, what other products can be used to satisfy the same need, how is the target offering different from the competitive offerings)
- Identify the characteristics of the other marketing mix variables (i.e., product, service, brand, incentives, communications, distribution)

⇨ **Step 2: Identify the key aspects of the price**

- Identify customers' willingness to pay for the set of benefits provided by the offering as well as customers' price sensitivity (i.e., the change in the quantity sold as a result of a change in price)
- Identify the pricing of competitive offerings and its impact on customer demand
- Identify the company's cost structure to determine the optimal price the company can charge to achieve its goals
- Identify the pricing of the offering to collaborators (e.g., distribution channels)

⇨ **Step 3: Design the implementation and control factors**

- Develop a plan to implement the proposed solution

- Design a mechanism to monitor progress and evaluate success

➲ *Developing an Incentives Strategy and Tactics*

Example: A car manufacturer is considering offering cash rebates to gain market share. What would you advise?

The key steps to developing a successful incentives strategy and tactics are:

⇨ **Step 1: Identify the underlying goal and strategy of the offering**

- Identify the goals to be achieved by the offering
- Identify the strategy adopted to achieve the goal (e.g., who are the target customers, what need does the offering satisfy, what other products can be used to satisfy the same need, how is the target offering different from the competitive offerings)
- Identify the characteristics of the other marketing mix variables (i.e., product, service, brand, price, communications, distribution)

⇨ **Step 2: Identify the key aspects of the incentives**

- Identify *customer incentives* (if any) to be offered with the new product/service (e.g., coupons, volume discounts, rebates, price reductions, contests, sweepstakes, and premiums)
- Identify the *collaborator incentives* (if any) to be offered with the new product/service (e.g., trade allowances, volume discounts, and co-op advertising allowances)
- Identify the *internal incentives* (if any) aimed at the company's employees (e.g., sales contests, awards, and bonuses)

⇨ **Step 3: Design the implementation and control factors**

- Develop a plan to implement the proposed solution
- Design a mechanism to monitor progress and evaluate success

➲ *Developing a Communications Strategy and Tactics*

Example: You are the CEO of a Fortune 500 company that is spending $500M on advertising each year. How do you know if this is a worthwhile investment? What would you do next year: would you increase the advertising budget, decrease it, or leave it unchanged?

The key steps to developing a successful pricing strategy and tactics are:

⇨ **Step 1: Identify the underlying goal and strategy of the offering**

- Identify the goals to be achieved by the offering
- Identify the strategy adopted to achieve the goal (e.g., who are the target customers, what need does the offering satisfy, what other products can be used to satisfy the same need, how is the target offering different from the competitive offerings)
- Identify the characteristics of the other marketing mix variables (i.e., product, service, brand, price, incentives, distribution)

⇨ **Step 2: Identify the key aspects of the communications**

- Identify communication *goals* (e.g., raise awareness, strengthen preferences, correct wrong impressions, etc.)
- Identify the *message* to be conveyed by the communications campaign (e.g., what are the benefits of the offering to target customers)
- Identify the campaign *budget*
- Identify the *media type(s)* to be used:
  - Advertising (e.g., TV, radio, Internet, newspapers, billboards, posters, in-store displays)
  - Direct marketing (catalogs, direct mail/email, telemarketing, Internet)
  - Public relations (e.g., newspaper, TV, radio coverage)

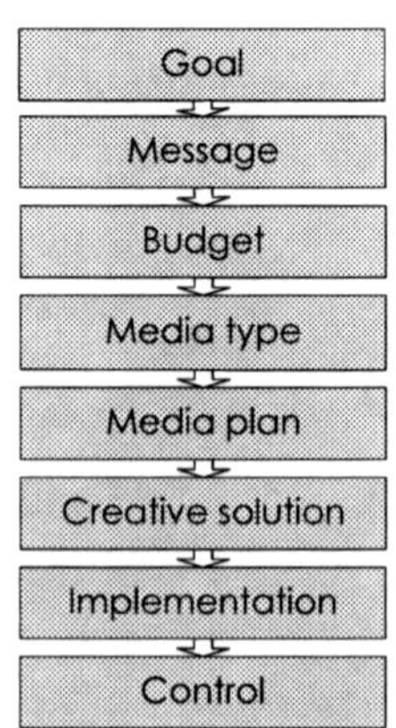

  - Event sponsorship, personal communications, product placement, etc.

- Develop a *media plan* identifying factors such as media schedule, timing of the campaign, and number of exposures

- Identify the *creative solution* (e.g., develop the story that best communicates the desired message)

✍ The communications *message* is typically outlined in the offering's positioning statement, which offers a succinct summary of the essence of the company's value proposition to target customers. The positioning statement identifies three main factors: (1) the target market (i.e., the customer segment targeted by the offering), (2) the frame of reference (i.e., how the customer should think about the offering: should the product be compared to a competitor's product or should it be described in terms of its inherent ability to meet a customer's need), and (3) the unique value proposition (i.e., the reason why customers will buy the offering, also referred to as point of difference).

⇨ **Step 3: Design the implementation and control factors**

- Develop a plan to implement the proposed solution

- Design a mechanism to monitor progress and evaluate success (e.g., awareness of the product, memorability of the campaign, sales impact, etc.)

➲ *Developing a Distribution Strategy and Tactics*

Example: An upscale ice-cream manufacturer is considering buying a fleet of refrigeration trucks to establish its own distribution system. Is this a good idea?

The key steps to developing a successful distribution strategy and tactics are:

⇨ **Step 1: Identify the underlying goal and strategy of the offering**

- Identify the goals to be achieved by the offering

- Identify the strategy adopted to achieve the goal (e.g., who are the target customers, what need does the offering satisfy, what other products can be used to satisfy the same need, how is the target offering different from the competitive offerings)

- Identify the characteristics of the other marketing mix variables (i.e., product, service, brand, price, incentives, communications)

⇨ **Step 2: Identify the key aspects of the distribution**

- Identify the essential aspects of the distribution strategy (e.g., breadth, depth, direct vs. indirect, etc.)
- Identify the channel partner compensation structure (e.g., margins, volume discounts, trade allowances, etc.)

⇨ **Step 3: Design the implementation and control factors**

- Develop a plan to implement the proposed solution
- Design a mechanism to monitor progress and evaluate success

3.3.3. Company-Focused Cases

Unlike offering-focused cases, which deal with issues concerning a particular offering, company-focused cases deal with issues on a more general, company level, which might involve managing multiple offerings and/or the overall company strategy. The three most common company-focused cases are: (1) developing a growth strategy for the entire company, (2) evaluating the viability of an acquisition and/or merger, and (3) evaluating the viability of entering or exiting an industry. These three scenarios are discussed in more detail below.

➲ *Developing a Growth Strategy for Company X*

Example: Develop a growth strategy for a large grocery store chain.

Growth-strategy cases can best be solved by using the revenue-growth framework outlined in the previous section. In particular, the following three issues should be addressed:

- Identify the market strategy (share-growth vs. market growth)

- Identify the customer strategy (current customers vs. new customers)
- Identify the product strategy (current products vs. new products)

➲ *Evaluating Viability of an Acquisition/Merger*

Example: Your client is trying to decide whether or not to invest in an office equipment company. Is this a good idea?

A relatively simple framework to evaluate the attractiveness of the acquired company and its fit with the acquiring company is the SWOT framework discussed in the previous section. In addition, the attractiveness of the industry in which the acquired company operates can be assessed using the Five Forces framework also addressed in the previous section.

➲ *Evaluating Industry Entry (Exit)*

Example: Your client, a cable company, is considering entering the home security market. What is your advice?

Cases involving evaluating the attractiveness of the entire industry can best be solved by using the Five Forces framework outlined in the previous section. The company's ability to compete in a particular industry also can be assessed by using the SWOT framework.

3.4. Planning Case Examples

- *Your client is considering launching a new product. Market data show that launching the product will decrease sales of an existing product by x%. Do you launch the product?*
- *We have many product upgrades, but it is hard to encourage customers to buy the new product because the original is still useful. How do you encourage customers to buy new upgrades of the product?*
- *You are charged with marketing a candy bar that has been very successful in France. What things should you consider in bringing the product to market in the United States?*
- *A large jeans manufacturing company is considering entering the upscale dress suit market to compete with the likes of Ralph Lauren, Burberry's, and Brooks Brothers. Is this a good idea? What issues do they need to consider?*
- *Should Coca-Cola add ice-cream to its product mix? If yes, how should it enter the ice-cream market?*
- *To increase its subscriber base, TiVo is considering giving a TiVo recorder to each customer who signs a two-year contract. What would you advise?*
- *Your client has asked you to help him optimize his product line. How do you approach this assignment?*
- *Your client, a large soft drink manufacturer, is considering switching from glass to plastic bottles. Is this a good idea?*
- *A start-up software company is preparing to launch its first product. How should they balance their customer service and sales force resources?*
- *Your client has developed a new statistical software package. How would you price it?*
- *A music company has asked your advice on how to price a soon-to-be released record of a new artist. How would you respond?*
- *A car manufacturer is considering reducing prices to gain market share. What do you tell him?*
- *Your client, Cingular Wireless, is trying to determine which customer segments it should target in order to increase revenues. What would you advise?*

3.5. Frameworks for Solving Performance-Gap Cases

A relatively simple and very useful approach for solving performance-gap cases is the Problem-Cause-Solution (P-C-S) framework. Unlike the G-S-T-I-C framework in which the primary focus is on formulating and implementing a new business program, the P-C-S framework is focused on identifying and rectifying problems in an existing program. The P-C-S analysis involves three key steps: formulating the problem, identifying its primary actionable cause, and developing a solution that eliminates the cause, thus solving the problem (Figure 3.7). These three steps are discussed in more detail below.

Figure 3.7. The P-C-S Framework

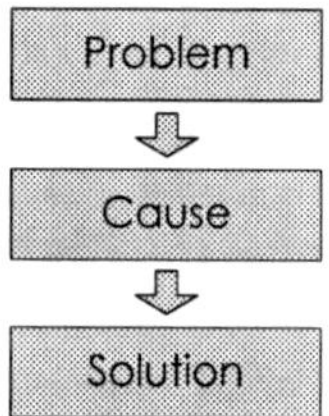

Step 1: Formulate the Problem

The first step in solving problem-based cases is to define the problem. In most cases, the problem can be defined by the presence of a *performance gap*: a discrepancy between the desired and the actual state of affairs, between the goal and the reality. To illustrate, profit-related problems typically reflect a discrepancy between the desired and the actual net income. Other common examples of performance gaps include discrepancies in net income, profit margins, revenues, and market share. Solving cases that involve complex problems comprising multiple aspects requires initial analysis to identify the key problem. This analysis involves breaking down complex problems into several simple ones and then prioritizing these simplified problems.

Step 2: Identify the Cause

The key to closing a performance gap is identifying its primary actionable cause. A cause is considered actionable if the company can act upon it and devise a solution to remove the cause. To illustrate, the fact that the economy is in a recession is not an actionable cause because the company cannot directly stimulate the economy. Other non-actionable causes include factors such as changes in consumer preferences, increasing competition, and various technological, social, legal, and political context factors. On the other hand, factors such as ineffective targeting, sub-optimal pricing, and inadequate promotion are actionable causes that could be readily removed by the company.

A useful approach to identifying the cause of the problem is exemplified by the G-S-T-I-C framework discussed earlier. In this context, the cause of the problem can be attributed to five main factors: unrealistic goal, inefficient strategy, sub-optimal tactics, poor implementation, and inadequate controls. These five factors are discussed in more detail below.

⇨ *Unrealistic Goals*

One potential cause for a company's inability to reach its goal is that the goal itself is unrealistic. To illustrate, a company's goal might include unreachable profitability, sales, and/or market share benchmarks. Unrealistic goals are often a result of biased expectations of management, stemming from strategic errors such as overestimating the overall size of the market, the speed of new product adoption, and/or customers' willingness to pay for the company's offering. Unrealistic goals can also result from a change in the environment in which the company operates. To illustrate, the market for the company's offering might be shrinking because of substitute technologies, profitability might be eroding in the face of increasing competition, and a sales decline might be attributed to a change in consumer preferences.

⇨ *Inefficient Strategy*

The cause of the company's problem can be also attributed to the inefficient strategy that the company follows to achieve its goal. In this context, most problems are likely to be associated with inferior value delivered to the relevant market players: target customers, the company, and its collaborators. To identify a potential cause, the manager needs to ensure that the offering does indeed fulfill customer needs better than the competitors' offerings, and does so in a way that enables the company and its collaborators to achieve their strategic goals.

In this context, there are three factors that could be the cause of the company's problem.

- *Inferior customer value.* The customer value gap might be caused by factors such as the inferiority of the offering value relative to the value delivered by competitors' offerings.
- *Inferior collaborator value.* The collaborator value gap might be caused by factors such as the inferiority of the offering margins relative to margins delivered by competitors' offerings.
- *Inferior company value.* The company value gap might stem from factors such as unprofitable cannibalization from a downscale line extension that steals share from other, more profitable offerings in the company's product line.

⇨ *Sub-optimal Tactics*

The cause for the company's problem can also be attributed to the tactical implementation of the offering. In this context, most marketing mistakes can be attributed to one or more of the following three types of value management failures: failure to create value, failure to communicate value, and failure to deliver value. These three factors are the cause of most breakdowns in the value-management process as follows:

- *Failure to create value.* Failure to create value for target customers, the company, and/or collaborators is among the most common reasons for an offering's failure. The failure to create value can often be attributed to factors such as an inferior product, inadequate service, unattractive or undifferentiated brand, inadequate pricing, and lack of or overreliance on incentives.
- *Failure to communicate value.* In addition to the failure to create value, a company can experience problems communicating its value proposition. The failure to communicate value can be attributed to factors such as ineffective advertising, public relations, product packaging, and in-store displays.
- *Failure to deliver value.* Another source of value mismanagement can be traced to the value-delivery process. To illustrate, a company's offering might not be readily available to customers because of inefficiencies in distribution chan-

nels or because of manufacturing constraints. (e.g., decreased shelf space, stock-outs).

⇨ ***Poor Implementation***

Another potential cause for a company's inability to reach its goal can be traced to poor implementation of the business plan. Even the best business plans fail when they are poorly implemented. Common implementation errors include incompetent project management, inefficient sales force, untrained customer service employees, and unforeseen logistical and technological difficulties. As a general rule, implementation cases are not very common in job interviews.

⇨ ***Inadequate Controls***

Inadequate controls can lead to two potential problems. The first possibility is that although the control measures indicate success, in reality the company has not achieved its goals. An example of such error is in using market share as a benchmark for success, even though the company's ultimate goal is net income. The second possibility is that the company is on the right track toward achieving its goals even though the controls are unable to detect it. In general, cases involving inadequate controls are not very common in job interviews.

Step 3: Propose a Solution

Once the primary actionable cause has been identified, the next step is to develop a solution that removes the cause and puts the company back on track toward achieving its goal. Identifying the primary cause is the key to solving the problem; the solution outlines a strategy to remove the readily identified cause. Depending on the nature of the problem, the solution might involve redefining the company's goal, developing a new strategy to achieve the company's existing goal, optimizing the tactics to implement the strategy, improving implementation, and/or verifying the controls.

The key principle in identifying a solution is that it should be directly linked to the readily identified primary actionable cause of the problem. Thus, if the primary cause of the company's inability to meet its benchmarks is that its goals are unrealistic, then the solution is to revise those goals and set new, more realistic goals. In the same vein, if the primary cause is inefficient strategy, then the solution will involve redesigning the existing strategy in a way that maximizes value to all relevant market participants (e.g., identifying new target markets, modifying the overall value proposition of the offering to customers, company, and/or its collaborators, and launching a new product). Similarly, if the problem has been attributed to sub-optimal tactics, then the solution needs to focus on optimizing the marketing mix variables. If the cause of the problem is poor implementation, then the solution needs to focus on improving the implementation. Finally, if the cause of the problem is using inadequate controls, then the solution needs to focus on developing adequate measurements to evaluate the company's progress towards its goals. The logic of identifying the solution in the context of the P-C-S and G-S-T-I-C frameworks is illustrated in Figure 3.8.

Figure 3.8. The P-C-S Framework

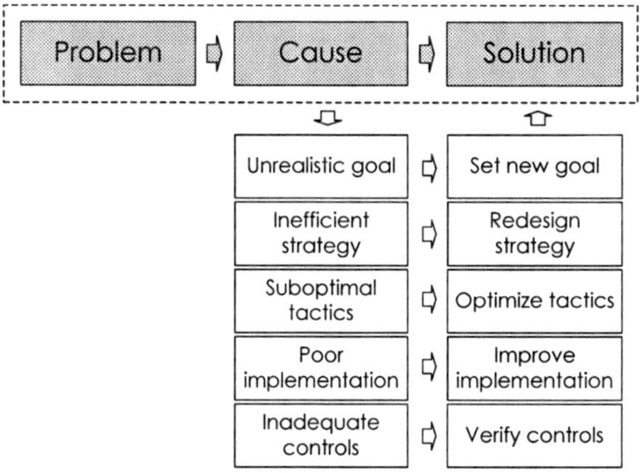

Problem ⇨ Cause ⇨ Solution

Cause		Solution
Unrealistic goal	⇨	Set new goal
Inefficient strategy	⇨	Redesign strategy
Suboptimal tactics	⇨	Optimize tactics
Poor implementation	⇨	Improve implementation
Inadequate controls	⇨	Verify controls

The P-C-S framework can be used for solving performance gap cases with varying scopes: from solving offering-specific performance gaps to solving gaps in the performance of the entire company. As the level of generality increases, the problem solving analysis also becomes increasingly complex, focusing on the interdependencies across different offerings and product lines.

3.6. General Solutions for Performance-Gap Cases

Performance-gap cases are often defined in terms of gaps in the value received by the company. It is often the case, however, that the cause of the company value gap can be related to a failure in delivering value to the other two key participants in the marketing exchange: the company's customers and collaborators. Therefore, performance gap analysis involves analyzing the three aspects of value, as defined by the three value factors: company value, customer value, and collaborator value (Figure 3.9). These three types of value gaps and the corresponding analyses are outlined in more detail below.

Figure 3.9. Performance Gap Analysis

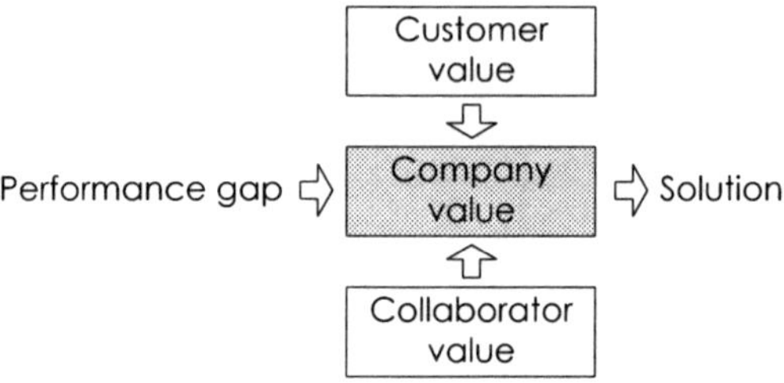

Company Value Analysis

Most company-related performance gaps can be readily identified using the company value framework introduced in the previous chapter (Figure 3.10). Strategies for closing the various types of company performance gaps are presented in a modular format. This modular approach allows breaking more complex gaps (e.g., profit, revenue, volume gaps) into relatively simpler problems that can be solved by applying relatively simple decision algorithms.

Figure 3.10. Performance Gaps: The Big Picture

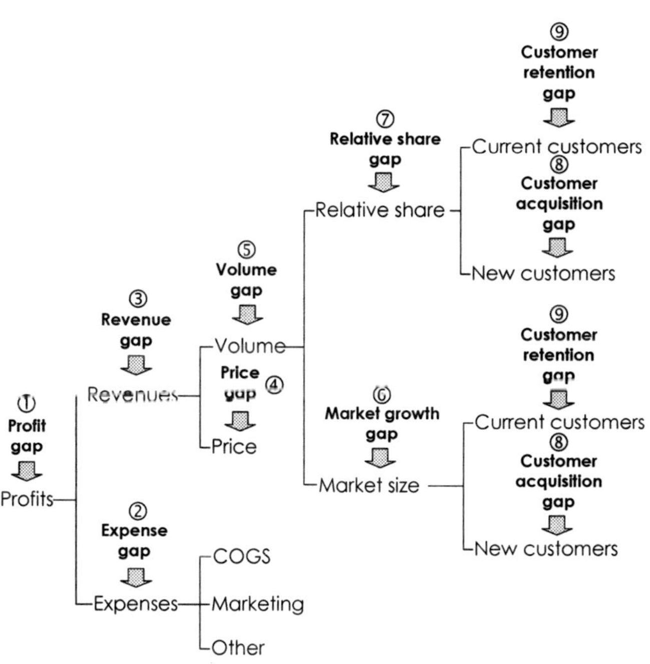

➲ *Closing a Profitability Gap ①*

Example: Your client would like to increase its profit margins by 6%. What would be your advice?

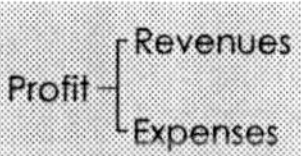

Identify the primary driver of the profitability gap: Determine whether the profitability gap can be attributed to an increase in expenses (expense gaps) or a decline in revenues (revenue gaps). Depending on the outcome, proceed to solve either the expense gap or the revenue gap (see ② and ③ below).

➲ *Closing an Expense Gap ②*

Example: Your profits are flat despite an increase in revenues. What is the problem and how would you remedy the situation?

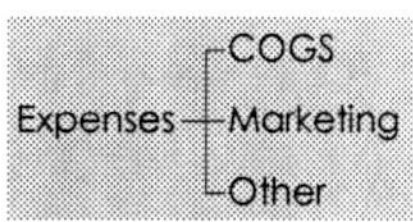

Identify the primary cause of the expense gap. Determine whether the expense gap can be attributed to one of three possible scenarios: an increase in costs of goods sold (Scenario A), an increase in marketing expenditures (Scenario B), or/and an increase in other expenses (Scenario C). Each of these three scenarios is discussed in more detail below.

⇨ **(A) Increased cost of goods sold (COGS).**

Identify the specific factor responsible for the incremental cost and seek solutions to reduce these costs. Some possible solutions include outsourcing, switching suppliers, optimizing operations, and adopting alternative technologies.

⇨ **(B) Increased marketing expenses.**

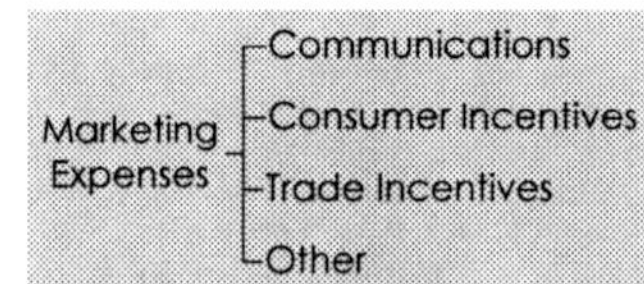

Identify the nature of the incremental marketing expenses. In particular, four main types of expenses can be identified: communication expenses (Scenario B1), consumer incentives (Scenario B2), trade incentives (Scenario B3), and miscellaneous other expenses (Scenario B4). Each of these four types of expenses is discussed in more detail below.

⇨ (B1) Increased communications costs.

- Identify the specifics of the increased communications costs. The most likely factor contributing to the increase in the communications costs is the increase in advertising expenditures.
- Evaluate the magnitude of the increase in the communications costs. Establish whether the increase in these costs could have contributed substantially to the increase in overall expenses.
- Evaluate the viability of the increase in the communications expenses. Are these incremental expenses a one-time factor or a recurring fact? How will these incremental costs impact profitability? If an increase in profitability is expected, establish when this would happen. If reducing advertising costs is a viable alternative, identify it as a possible solution and proceed to analyze the other factors.

✍ When assessing advertising costs, keep in mind that:

- For mature products, the impact of communication expenditures on company revenues is not immediate.

It often takes months to observe a significant increase in sales.

- In many cases, there is a diminishing return on advertising expenditures. Adding $10M to a $100M advertising budget might have a lesser impact on sales than adding $10M to a $5M budget. Also, $10M spent on advertising a well-known brand might have a lesser impact on sales than $10M spent on advertising a lesser known brand.
- Most of the communications expenditures are fixed costs; they do not depend on the number of units sold. Note, however, that even though their absolute size remains unchanged regardless of the output volume, advertising costs become progressively smaller per unit of output as volume increases (because the fixed costs are allocated over a larger number of output units).

⇨ (B2) Increased cost of consumer incentives

- Identify the specifics of the increase in costs of consumer incentives. The most likely factors contributing to the rising cost of consumer incentives are the increased cost of coupons, volume discounts, rebates, price reductions, contests, sweepstakes, and premiums.
- Evaluate the impact of the increase in the cost of incentives on total costs. Establish whether the increase in these costs could have contributed substantially to the increase in overall expenses.
- Evaluate the viability of the increase in costs of incentives. Establish the logic, the magnitude, and the timeframe as to how these incremental costs will impact profitability. If reducing the cost of consumer incentives is a viable alternative, identify it as a possible solution and proceed to analyze the other factors.

✍ When assessing consumer incentives keep in mind that:

- Although sales promotions in most cases lead to an increase in the sales volume, incremental sales are often not sufficient to compensate for the costs of incentives. Nevertheless, many companies continue to use sales promotions to counter similar incentives from competitors.

- Coupons are primarily used for price discrimination in order to selectively target price-sensitive consumers.

- Because the basic premise of customer incentives is to increase sales volume by enhancing the value of the offering to the customer, communications (e.g., advertising) are an integral component of consumer incentive programs. Indeed, without promoting the incentive to customers, only customers who would have purchased the offering anyway would take advantage of the incentives, which would add to the company's costs without increasing revenues.

- Most incentives (e.g., price reductions, coupons, rebates, premiums) are variable costs and, unlike communications, increasing sales volume will not diminish the per-unit cost of the incentives.

⇨ (B3) Increased cost of trade incentives

- Identify the specifics of the increased trade incentives costs. The most likely factors contributing to the increase in the cost of trade incentives are: trade allowances, volume discounts, and co-op advertising allowances.

- Evaluate the magnitude of the increase in the costs of incentives and establish whether the increase in these costs could have contributed substantially to the increase in overall expenses.

- Evaluate the rationale for increasing the costs of incentives. Establish the logic, the magnitude, and the timeframe as to how these incremental costs will impact profitability. If reducing the cost of trade incentives is a viable alternative, identify it as a possible solution and proceed to analyze the other factors.

✍ When assessing trade incentives, keep in mind that because of a shift of power from manufacturers to retailers, trade incentives account for a substantial portion of a company's marketing expenses. Thus, across industries, the average split of the promotional budget between communications (e.g., advertising) and incentives (e.g., trade incentives) is close to 30/70 in favor of incentives.

⇨ (B4) Increase of other marketing costs

- Identify the primary cause for the increased marketing costs. Among factors most likely to contribute to the increase in the cost of business incentives are: sales force, marketing research, and marketing overhead.
- Identify the nature of the increased costs and evaluate their magnitude. Establish whether the increase in these costs could have contributed substantially to the increase in overall expenses.
- Evaluate the rationale for the cost increase. Establish the logic, the magnitude, and the timeframe as to how these incremental costs will impact profitability. If reducing these costs is a viable alternative, identify it as a possible solution and proceed to analyze the other factors.

⇨ **(C)** Other expenses

- Determine the primary cause for the incremental costs. The most likely factors contributing to the cost increase are: capital expenses, administrative expenses, sales force, research and development expenses, etc.
- Identify specific solutions to reduce costs by eliminating their primary source.

➲ *Closing a Revenue Gap* ③

Example: Your sales revenues have been declining over the past year. How would you address that?

Identify the primary cause of the revenue gap. Determine whether the revenue gap is caused by a decrease in price (Scenario A) or a decrease in the sales volume (Scenario B).

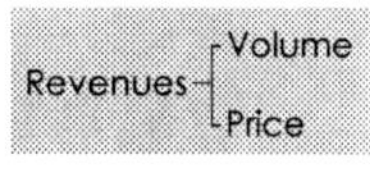

⇨ **Scenario A.** The revenue gap is caused by under pricing

Evaluate the reasons for maintaining a relatively low price (see ④ below).

⇨ **Scenario B.** The revenue gap is caused by a decrease in sales volume

Evaluate the reasons for the decrease in sales volume (see ⑤ below).

➲ *Closing a Price Gap ④*

Example: Your client is considering raising the price of its best-selling product in order to meet its profit goals. Is this a good idea?

Evaluate the rationale for maintaining a relatively low price. In the absence of a valid reason for the low price, a price increase might be a potential strategy to close the revenue gap. If there was a valid reason for maintaining a low price (e.g., the company with a commodity product facing intensifying price competition) then proceed with the analysis and seek alternative solutions.

✍ When assessing the impact of price on revenues and profitability, keep in mind that raising the price does not always increase profitability. In product categories where demand is elastic, a price increase might lead to a sizable decline in sales, such that the loss of revenues due to the decline in sales volume could be greater than the revenue gain from the price increase.

➲ *Closing a Sales Volume Gap ⑤*

Example: Your client, McDonald's, is concerned that their growth has been slower than expected. How would you advise them?

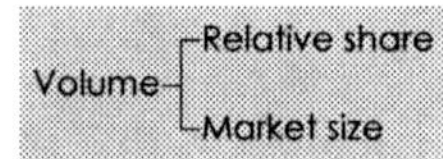

Determine whether the sales volume gap can be attributed to a decline in the relative share of the company vis-à-vis the competition or if it is a non-company-specific, industry-wide phenomenon.

⇨ **(A)** Relative share decline

Evaluate the cause for the decline in the relative share of the company's offering (see ⑦ below).

⇨ **(B)** Market size decline

Evaluate the cause for the market decline (see ⑥ below).

➲ *Closing a Market Growth Gap* ⑥

Example: Your client, Eastman Kodak Company, is facing declining sales of its traditional film products due to the growth of digital photography. What would you advise?

Determine whether the primary source of the market growth gap is a decline in sales volume from current customers or if it is a decline in the rate of acquiring new customers (as when analyzing the relative share gap).

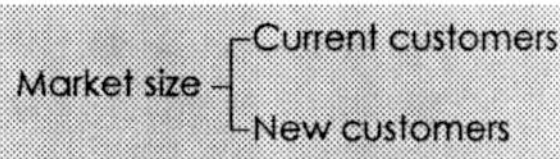

⇨ **(A)** Decline of sales to current customers

Evaluate the cause for the decline of sales to current customers (see the customer retention gap analysis).

⇨ **(B)** Decline in the rate of acquiring new customers

Evaluate the cause for the decline in the customer acquisition rate (see the customer acquisition gap analysis).

➲ *Closing a Relative Share Gap* ⑦

Example: Your market share has been declining for the past year. What would you do?

The relative share gap reflects a scenario in which the company is losing relative share to the competition. This can happen in a declining market (i.e., the company is losing share to the competition, whose sales volume is also declining, albeit at a slower rate) as well as in a growing market (i.e., the company is gaining share at a lower rate than the overall market growth).

Determine whether the share gap can be attributed to a decline in the sales volume from current customers or if is caused by a decline in the rate of acquiring new customers.

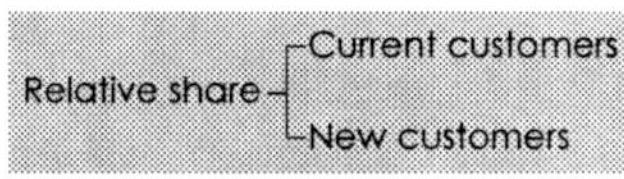

⇨ **(A)** Decline of sales to current customers

Evaluate the cause for the decline of sales to current customers (see ⑨ below).

⇨ **(B)** Decline in the rate of acquiring new customers

Evaluate the cause for the decline in the customer acquisition rate (see ⑧ below).

➲ *Closing a Customer Acquisition Gap* ⑧

Example: Your client, a major satellite radio company, has a problem attracting new customers. What would you advise?

Determine the cause of the declining rate of acquiring new customers. Similar to the customer retention gap, in most cases, the cause of low customer acquisition rates can be linked to breakdowns in the value-delivery process (see customer value analysis in the next section).

➲ *Closing a Customer Retention Gap* ⑨

Example: Your client, a major retail broker, is faced with a declining customer base. How would you address this problem?

Determine the cause of customer attrition. In most cases, the cause of customer attrition can be linked to breakdowns in the value-delivery process (see customer value analysis in the next section).

Customer Value Analysis

➲ *Closing a Customer Value Gap* ⑧⑨

Example: Your client has a problem growing (retaining) its customer base. What would you advise?

Most customer value gaps can be linked to one of the three aspects of value management: creating value, communicating value, and delivering value. From a customer perspective, these three value-management aspects translate into three key factors that ensure the success of an offering: attractiveness, awareness, and availability. Thus, customers should be aware of the offering, find the offering attractive, and have access to the offering, which should be readily available for purchase/consumption.

⇨ **Step 1.** Evaluate the offering's *attractiveness* to customers.

Identify the key benefits and costs associated with the offering. The goal is to determine how the key value-related marketing mix variables (i.e., product, service, brand, price, incentives) translate into utility to the customer.

When evaluating the overall attractiveness of an offering to its target customers, one should ask three key questions: (1)

Is the offering inherently attractive to customers; that is, in the absence of competitive products, would the target customer buy the product/service? (2) How does this offering compare to competitors' offerings? (3) If the offering is part of a product line launched by the same company, how does it compare to the company's other offerings? Potential improvements that enhance the attractiveness of an offering involve changes in the product, service, brand, price, and/or incentives.

⇨ **Step 2.** Evaluate customers' *awareness* of the offering.

Determine whether customers are aware of the offering and whether they understand the benefits and costs associated with the offering. If the awareness level of the offering among target customers is low, then the solution is to promote the offering using an optimal mix of various communication tools: advertising, public relations, personal selling, online communications, in-store displays, packaging, product placement, event marketing, etc.

It is also possible that even though the majority of the target customers are aware of the offering, they might be unclear or have a wrong impression about the benefits and costs of the offering. In this case, the solution is to reposition the offering to more clearly communicate its value to customers.

⇨ **Step 3.** Evaluate the offering's *availability* to customers.

In many cases, a company's distribution strategy may be negatively influenced by a variety of factors such as inadequate geographical coverage (e.g., the offering is not available in the areas where target customers live/shop), stock-outs that result from underestimating customer demand, and/or sub-par logistics of the distribution channel. The solution is to remove the cause of the distribution gap and improve both the geographical coverage and the logistics to eliminate stock-outs, etc.

Collaborator Value Analysis

➲ *Closing a Collaborator Value Gap*

Example: Your client, a large computer game manufacturer, has a difficult time convincing software programmers to develop games for its platform. How would you address this problem?

Although not very common, some cases involve problems stemming from a performance gap concerning one or more of the company's collaborators. The general approach to solving such problems is to use cost-benefit analysis, similar to that used in customer analysis. The basic idea is to identify the cause of the problem from a collaborator's standpoint by evaluating the benefits and the costs of the offering to collaborators and then relate the value of the offering to collaborators' goals.

3.7. Performance-Gap Case Examples

- *A computer manufacturer is experiencing declining sales. Its product is superior in lifetime and quality to its competitors' products. What would you do?*
- *A shoe manufacturer is gaining market share but has experienced declining profits. What would you do?*
- *You are a product manager for product X. For the past few years, the share of your company has been decreasing even though the overall category was flat. What would you do?*
- *You are the brand manager of a product whose sales have been flat for the last five years. However, the brand's market share has been growing by 5% per year. What's happening with this particular brand and what would you do about it?*
- *Your brand has experienced substantial share erosion for the past several years because of a competitor that claims to be "better." Under what circumstances should you reformulate your product?*
- *A company's market share is decreasing and the two options on the table are to lower the price or to advertise. What would you do?*
- *Your client is a high-end sports car manufacturer who is concerned about vulnerability to market cycles. What is your advice?*
- *You are the CEO of a large software company. You notice that one of your software products is losing money. What would you do?*
- *Your client, the leading soft drink manufacturer in Brazil, is losing share to one of its competitors. How would you advise your client?*
- *Your client is losing money because of the large number of incoming customer calls. What would you advise?*
- *You are the director of the San Francisco Opera. Ticket sales are down. What would you do?*

3.8. Frameworks for Solving External-Change Cases

This type of case involves evaluating the impact of a significant change in the context in which the company operates. In general, there are four main types of external changes that affect the company and/or its offerings. These four external factors can be derived from the 5-C framework: changes in the customer base (e.g., changes in customer demographics, buying power, needs and preferences), changes in the competitive environment (e.g., a new competitive entry or a change in the strategic and/or tactical aspects of a competitive offering, such as adding new product features, lowering price, launching an aggressive advertising campaign); changes in collaborators' behavior; and finally, changes in the social, political, technological, legal, and economic context.

The key to solving external-change cases is evaluating the impact of the external change on the company's current activities. This implies that to evaluate the impact of a change in the environment, the key is to understand the company's business plan before the external change and then determine what adjustments have to be made so that the company can successfully operate in the new environment.

One approach to solving this type of case involves using the G-S-T-I-C framework to estimate the impact of external factors on the company's activities. In this context, the goal is to identify the potential changes in the company's goal, strategy, tactics, implementation, and/or control activities caused by the external factors and then make the corresponding adjustments. This approach is visualized in Figure 3.11.

Figure 3.11. Using the G-S-T-I-C Framework to Solve External-Change Cases

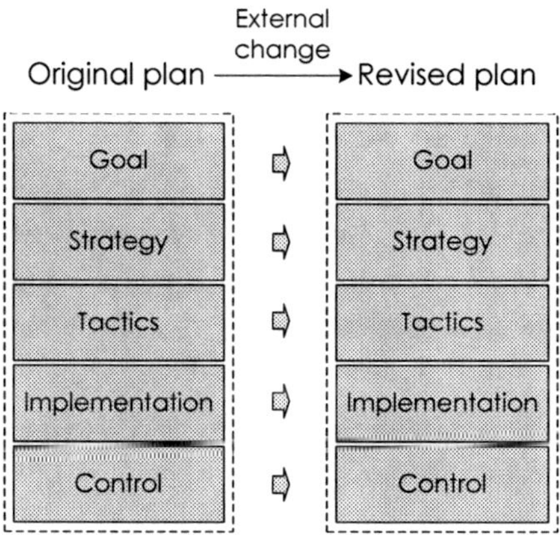

This approach can be used for solving external-change cases with different scopes: from evaluating offering-specific external changes to evaluating the impact of external changes on the performance of the entire company. As the level of generality increases, the evaluation also becomes increasingly complex, focusing on the inter-dependencies across different offerings and product lines.

3.9. General Solutions for External-Change Cases

Cases involving a change in the environment can be best solved by using the following three-step approach.

⇨ **Step 1.** Identify the specifics of the external change.

For example, if the change involves a competitive price reduction, investigate the depth and duration of the price reduction. If the change involves an aggressive competitive advertising campaign, find out more details about factors such as message, frequency, and coverage.

⇨ **Step 2.** Evaluate the impact of the external change on the offering and/or the company.

For example, evaluate the impact of a competitor's lower price on the success of the company's offering and the company's ability to achieve its goals.

⇨ **Step 3.** Identify the optimal response and revise the company's business plan accordingly.

Make the necessary adjustments to the company's business plan as reflected in the G-S-T-I-C framework. These adjustments might include revising the company's goal, repositioning its strategy, redesigning its tactics, developing an alternative implementation plan and/or identifying a new set of control benchmarks.

3.10. External-Change Case Examples

- *Your competitor just lowered its price. What do you do?*
- *Your competitor just launched an aggressive advertising campaign. What do you do?*
- *What would you do if R&D told you that they had come up with a pasta sauce that lowers cholesterol?*
- *How should Fatburger (fast food chain) react to consumers' obsession with fat-free food?*
- *How should Segway react to state laws restricting the use of Segways on sidewalks?*
- *Your client, a large sports club, is successfully operating in an upscale urban neighborhood. A developer announces plans to build a residential complex nearby that will also include a sports club that will directly compete with your client's club. How would you advise your client?*
- *What is the impact of raising gasoline prices on McDonald's sales?*

3.11. Solving Audit Cases

While most of the marketing cases present a problem (planning, performance gap, or external change) in search of a solution, some cases also include one or more potential solutions, asking managers to audit the viability of the proposed solutions and either choose one of the available options or propose a better solution. To illustrate, a case might involve evaluating the viability of launching an aggressive advertising campaign to promote a new offering, evaluating the viability of introducing sales promotions to increase the market share of a product line, as well as the viability of a company's decision to lower prices in response to a new competitive entry.

The key to analyzing audit cases with readily identified solutions is to evaluate the proposed option not simply by evaluating its pros and cons but also by identifying alternative strategies for solving the underlying problem and comparing it to these strategies. A relatively simple yet effective strategy for solving action-auditing cases involves the following four steps:

Step 1: Identify the goal to be achieved (or the problem to be solved) by the proposed action.

Step 2: Identify the strengths (benefits) and weaknesses (costs) of the proposed action with respect to achieving this goal.

Step 3: Identify the alternative actions to achieve the company's goal.

Step 4: Evaluate the relative advantages and disadvantages of the proposed action vis-à-vis the alternative actions.

The logic for the proposed four-step analysis is outlined in Figure 3.12. The two important analyses here are the cost-benefit analysis and the relative advantage analysis. The cost-benefit analysis examines whether the strengths of the proposed solution outweigh its weaknesses with respect to achieving the company's ultimate goal. The relative advantage analysis further examines the benefits of the proposed action vis-à-vis the alternative solutions that could be used to achieve the company's goal.

Figure 3.12. The Framework for Solving Audit cases

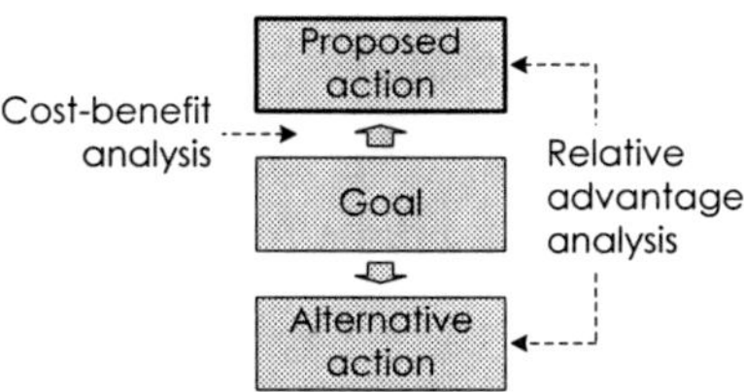

In this context, analyzing cases with readily identified solutions is not much different from analyzing cases without proposed solutions. The key difference is that, in addition to developing potential solutions, cases with proposed solutions also require comparing these potential solutions with the solution readily identified in the case.

In general, cases with readily identified solutions are very common both in case interviews and in reality. Indeed, when faced with a problem, managers often have an inclination to adopt a certain course of action, sometimes without considering all potential alternatives. As a result, the solutions proposed by these managers are often sub-optimal and could be easily discredited by the alternative solutions offered by other managers and/or consultants. Only by evaluating the pros and cons of their proposed actions vis-à-vis the alternative solutions can a manger develop a successful solution to the company's problem.

3.12. Audit Case Examples

- *A fast-food chain is considering lowering prices to improve its bottom line. Is this a good idea?*
- *A small software company is considering launching its new product by advertising during the Super Bowl. What would be your advice?*
- *Your client has to decide whether to acquire a sports drink company. Advise your client on the viability of his acquisition strategy.*
- *A large credit card company is considering outsourcing some of its operations abroad. What would you advise?*
- *Your client, a major online content provider, is considering introducing a new pricing structure, which implies annual price increases. Is this a good idea?*
- *Your client, a major pharmaceutical company, has invented a drug that is twice as effective in curing lung cancer as the best drug currently on the market. You are asked to help develop a pricing strategy for the drug. How would you approach the assignment?*
- *A major European airline is thinking about lowering its fares to better compete with discount carriers. Is this a good idea?*
- *Company X wants to increase the market share of its flagship product so that it can claim that its product has the largest customer base. What would you advise so that the company can reach its goal?*
- *Your client is ready to launch a new product that is both a pen and a USB flash drive. Should he distribute this product to office supply stores or to computer stores?*
- *Your client must build a new computer chip manufacturing plant. You must decide in which country to build the plant. What factors would you consider?*
- *The CEO of a start-up biotech company has asked your advice in developing a business plan. How would you approach this assignment?*
- *A solar panel manufacturer is contemplating adding capacity. Is this a good idea?*

Part II: References

Chapter 4: Concepts

4.1. Key Marketing Concepts

Advertising Allowance: A form of trade promotion in which retailers are given a discount in exchange for promoting the product in their own advertising (see also *promotional allowance*).

Affiliate Marketing: A marketing strategy that involves revenue sharing between online advertisers/merchants and online publishers/salespeople. Compensation is typically awarded based on performance measures such as sales, click-throughs, registrations, or a combination of factors.

Ansoff Matrix: see *product-market growth matrix.*

Awareness Rate: The number of customers who are aware of the offering, relative to the total number of potential customers.

Baby Boomers: Age-defined market segment most often used in reference to Americans born between 1946 and 1964 (see also *Generation X* and *Generation Y*).

Backward Integration: A form of *vertical integration* that involves upstream expansion of the supply chain.

BCG Matrix: *Portfolio model* developed by the Boston Consulting Group to guide cash allocation decisions across different *strategic business units* of a company (see *BCG framework*).

Brand Audit: A comprehensive analysis of a brand, most often to determine the sources of brand equity.[1]

Brand Equity: The value of the brand. Brand equity can be evaluated in two contexts: from the company's point of view (company-based brand equity) and from the customers' point of view (customer-based brand equity). From a company's perspective, brand equity reflects the financial outcome from brand ownership, as well as management's ability to leverage the brand. In this context, brand equity determines the premium that should be placed on a company's valuation because of brand ownership. From a customer's perspective, brand equity is defined as the differential impact of brand knowledge on consumer response to an offering's marketing efforts.[2] Thus, a brand has positive equity when consumers react more favorably to the various aspects of an offering (i.e., product, service, price, incentives, communications, and distribution) when the brand is identified relative to when it is not identified. In this context, one of the key aspects of brand equity is the price premium customers are willing to pay for the branded (vis-à-vis the identical unbranded) product. Other dimensions of brand equity include enhanced perceptions of product performance, less vulnerability to service inconsistencies, more elastic response to price promotions, greater communications effectiveness, and increased channel power.

Brand Extension: The strategy of using the same brand name in a different context (e.g., different product category or different price tier). There are two main types of brand extensions: within-category extensions and cross-category extensions. In within-category brand extensions, the same brand name is applied to several products within the same product category. In contrast, in cross-category brand extensions the same brand name is applied to products in different categories. To illustrate, extending the Starbucks name to different coffee flavors is typically referred to as a within-category (or line-based) brand extension; whereas, extending it to ice cream is considered a cross-category brand extension.

Brand: A marketing device designed (1) to identify a company and/or a company's offering, (2) to differentiate it from the competition, and (3) to create value for the company and the customer. The most common brand elements include the brand name, logo, symbol, character, jingle, and slogan.

Bundling: Combining multiple offerings.

Cannibalization: Scenario in which a newly introduced offering steals share from other offering(s) within the same company. To illustrate, the introduction of Vanilla Coke cannibalized the sales of Coca-Cola Classic. Cannibalization is not necessarily "bad" for the company. In many cases cannibalization can have an overall positive impact (e.g., when the margins of the new offering are higher than that of the cannibalized one, or when the new offering seeks to achieve different strategic goals).

Captive Pricing: see *complementary pricing.*

Category Killers: Specialty retailers that focus on one product category such as electronics or business supplies at very competitive prices (e.g., Home Depot, Office Depot, CompUSA).

Channel Conflict: Tension between members of a *distribution channel,* often caused by different profit optimization strategies of each channel member. There are three types of channel conflicts: *vertical, horizontal,* and *multichannel.*

Channel Member: A participant (e.g., a wholesaler, a retailer) in the *distribution channel.*

Channel Power: The ability of one channel member to get another channel member to do what it otherwise would not have done (e.g., a retailer allocating premium shelf space to a given manufacturer's products without being explicitly compensated for it).[3]

Co-branding: Joint marketing strategy that involves using multiple brand names in a single offering (e.g., United Airlines Mileage Plus Visa credit card, Nike Air Jordan products).

Comparative Advertising: Advertising strategy whereby a given offering is directly compared to another offering.

Competitive Parity Budgeting: Marketing strategy based on (1) matching the competitors' absolute level of spending or (2) the proportion per point of market share.

Complementary Pricing: Pricing strategy applicable to uniquely compatible, multi-part offerings, whereby a company charges a low (relative to its cost) introductory price on the first part and higher prices for the other parts. Classic examples include razors and blades, printers and cartridges, cell phones and cell phone service, etc. Note that the unique compatibility is crucial to the success of complementary pricing: Only the printer manufacturer should sell cartridges that fit in its printers (also known as *two-part pricing, captive pricing*).

Complementors: Companies that offer complementary products and/or services without directly collaborating with the company delivering the core offering[4] (e.g., Belkin manufacturing accessories for Apple's iPod without directly collaborating with Apple).

Consumer Promotions: Promotion activities aimed at the consumer (rather than the retailer). Typical consumer promotional activities include free samples, coupons, rebates, point-of-purchase displays, etc.

Continuity Programs: Promotional activities used to encourage and reward repeat purchases by acknowledging each purchase made by a consumer and offering a premium as purchases accumulate (e.g. frequent-flyer programs).

Contractual Vertical Marketing System: Channel structure whereby the relationships between the manufacturer and the distributor are set on a contractual basis (rather than a common ownership – see also *corporate vertical marketing system*).

Cooperative Advertising: Advertising strategy in which a manufacturer and a retailer jointly advertise their offering to consumers. In this case, the manufacturer pays a portion of a retailer's advertising costs in return for featuring its products/services.

Copyright: A legal term describing rights given to creators for their literary and artistic works. The types of works covered by copyright include: literary works such as novels, poems, plays, reference works, newspapers and computer programs; databases; films, musical compositions, and choreography; artistic works such as paintings, drawings, photographs and sculpture; architecture; and advertisements, maps and technical drawings.

Corporate Vertical Marketing System: Channel structure whereby the manufacturer and the distributor have common ownership (rather than a contractual relationship – see also *contractual vertical marketing system*).

Cost-Plus Pricing: A pricing method in which the final price is determined by adding a fixed mark-up to the costs of the product. It is easy to calculate and is commonly used in industries where profit margins are relatively stable. Its key drawback is that it does not take into account customer demand and competitive pricing.

Customer Management Audit: A comprehensive analysis of a company's customer management strategy.

Customer Equity: The lifetime value of a company's customers.

Deceptive Pricing: A strategy that involves presenting an offering's price to the buyer in a way that is deliberately misleading.

Delphi Method: A method of forecasting that relies on expert opinion. The method is named after the site of the most revered oracle in ancient Greece, who made predictions at the Temple of Apollo in Delphi. The Delphi method typically involves answering a set of specific questions by a panel of experts.

Detailers: Indirect sales force promoting pharmaceuticals to doctors and pharmacists so that they, in turn, recommend the brand to the consumer.

Direct Channel: Distribution strategy in which the manufacturer and the end-customer interact directly with each other without intermediaries (see also *indirect channel* and *hybrid channel*).

Distribution Channel: A way of delivering a company's offering to its customers.

Diversification: A market growth strategy aimed at developing offerings that are new to the company and introducing those offerings to customers not currently served by the company (e.g., entertainment offerings by Vivendi Universal, originally Compagnie Générale des Eaux, a French water company; see *product-market growth framework*).

Economies of Scale: An inverse relationship between the scale of production and the marginal production costs. Thus, if the marginal production costs do not vary as a function of the output volume, there are no economies of scale. If, however, marginal production costs decrease with the increase in the production output, then this increase reflects the economies of scale. By the same logic, if an increase in the production output results in an increase in the marginal production costs, then this decrease reflects diseconomies of scale. Thus, for a given company, the marginal production costs decrease until they reach a certain minimum (economies of scale), then increase as the firm size increases further (diseconomies of scale).

Everyday Low Pricing (EDLP): Pricing strategy whereby a retailer maintains low prices without frequent price promotions.

Experience Curve: The curve describing how costs of production decline as cumulative output increases over time. The concept was introduced by the Boston Consulting Group in 1966 to describe the finding that costs decline approximately 20 to 30% in real terms each time accumulated experience doubles.[5] At present, the term experience curve is used in a more general sense to capture the notion that costs tend to decrease with experience. Often used interchangeably with *learning curve.*

Experience Curve Pricing: Pricing strategy based on an anticipated future lower cost structure resulting from scale economies and experience curve effects.

Extension: A strategy whereby a company adds a new offering to its current product line, thus extending the assortment of its products and services. The key reason for extending an existing offering is to develop a new value proposition to better address the needs of a specific customer segment. Two types of extensions are commonly distinguished: *horizontal* and *vertical*.

Fighting Brand: Strategic (most often downscale) product extension to confront lower priced competitor(s).

Five Forces of Competition: A concept and framework advanced by Michael Porter[6] for analyzing the nature of the competition on an industry level.

Focus Group: A sample of people, usually representative of a particular customer segment, that is of interest to the company. Also used in reference to a method in which focus group participants are engaged in unstructured discussions – typically moderated by a facilitator – aimed at revealing insights, ideas, and observations on a particular topic.

Forward Buying: Increasing the channel inventory (also referred to as "channel stuffing"), usually to take advantage of a manufacturer's promotion and/or in anticipation of price increases.

Forward Integration: A form of *vertical integration* that involves downstream expansion of the supply chain (e.g., a manufacturer establishing its own distribution system).

Generation X: Age-defined market segment most often used in reference to Americans born between 1964 and 1975 (see also *Baby Boomers* and *Generation Y*).

Generation Y: Age-defined market segment most often used in reference to Americans born between 1976 and 1999 (other commonly used ranges are 1981–1995 and 1979–1994). Nearly 60 million people belong to this group, which is three times the size of *Generation X* and is the largest age-derived segment (see also *Baby Boomers).*

General Electric Matrix: *Portfolio model* developed by General Electric to guide cash allocation decisions across different *strategic business units* of a company (see *GE framework).*

Gray Market: A market in which products are sold through unauthorized channels of distribution.

Heterogeneous Market: A scenario in which customers vary in their response to a company's offering (see also *homogeneous market*).

Homogeneous Market: A scenario in which all customers are likely to react in a very similar manner with respect to a company's offering (e.g., they like the same combination of product and service features, are willing to pay a similar price for a given offering, are likely to respond to a company's promotional activities in a similar manner, can be reached through the same communication means, have access to the offering through the same distribution channels, etc.) See also *heterogeneous market.*

Horizontal Channel Conflict: A conflict between members within the same level of the channel (e.g., retailer – retailer). Horizontal conflicts occur when different channels target the same customer segment with identical or substitutable offerings (e.g., different retailers selling the same product to the same customer). See also *channel conflict.*

Horizontal Extension: An *extension* in which the price is not the key differentiating factor between the original and the extended offering (Figure 4.1). To illustrate, different yogurt flavors, different types of cola (regular, cherry, vanilla, diet, caffeine-free) would be considered horizontal extensions (see also *extension, vertical extension*).

Figure 4.1. Horizontal Extension

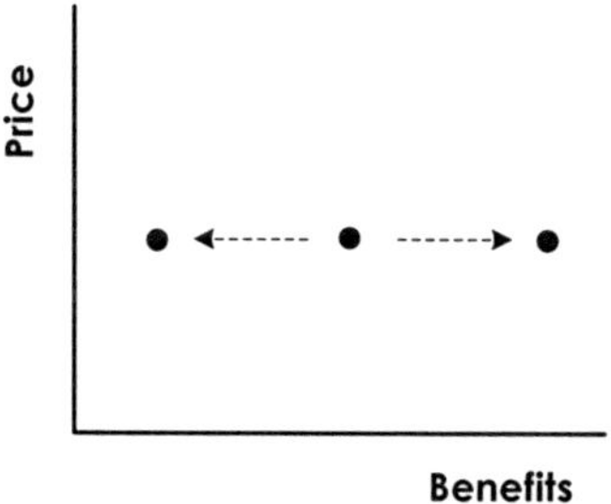

Horizontal Price Fixing: The (illegal) practice whereby competitors explicitly or implicitly collaborate to set prices (see also *vertical price fixing*).

Hybrid Channel: Distribution strategy in which the manufacturer and the end-customer interact with each other through multiple channels – for example, directly and through intermediaries such as wholesalers and/or retailers (Figure 4.2; see also *direct channel* and *indirect channel*).

Figure 4.2. Hybrid Channel

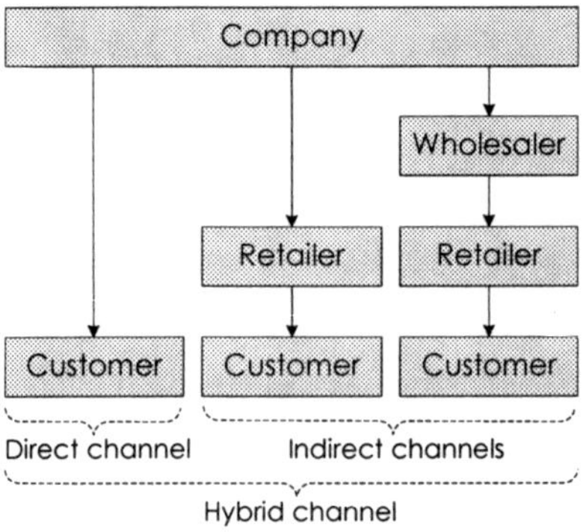

Image Pricing: see *price signaling.*

Impression: A single exposure of an ad to one person.

Indirect Channel: Distribution strategy in which the manufacturer and the end-customer interact with each other through intermediaries such as wholesalers and/or retailers (see also *direct channel* and *hybrid channel*).

Institutional Advertising: Advertising strategy designed to build goodwill or an image for an organization (rather than to promote specific goods or services).

Integrated Marketing Communications (IMC): The strategy of designing marketing communications programs to coordinate all communication activities (e.g., advertising, public relations, personal selling) to provide a consistent message across different communication channels.

Learning Curve: The curve describing how labor costs of production decline as cumulative output increases over time. The logic behind the concept of a learning curve is that labor hours per unit decline on repetitive tasks. The term learning curve is often used interchangeably with the more general concept of experience curve, although an argument has been made to differentiate the two concepts.[7]

Loss Leadership: Pricing strategy that involves setting a low price (often at or below cost) in an attempt to increase the sales of other products and services (e.g., a retailer sets the price low on a popular item in an attempt to build store traffic, thus increasing the sales of other, more profitable items).

Manufacturer's Advertised Price (MAP): Pricing strategy in which the manufacturer sets a recommended retail price and offers incentives to encourage retailers not to undercut the recommended price. To illustrate, a common strategy to ensure channel cooperation are advertising allowances that reimburse the retailer for co-op advertising only if the retail price does not drop below a specified level. MAP is typically used to reduce multi-channel conflict by establishing a price floor to control underpricing.

Market-Development Strategy: A market growth strategy aimed at acquiring new customers for a company's current offerings.

Market Potential: Maximum total of sales of a product/service by all firms.

Market Share: A brand's share of the total sales of all offerings within the product category in which the brand competes. Market share is determined by dividing a brand's sales volume by the total category sales volume, where sales can be defined in terms of revenues or on a unit basis (e.g., number of items sold or number of customers served).

$$\text{Market share} = \frac{\text{An offering's sales in market X}}{\text{Total sales in market X}}$$

Market Structure Analysis: An analysis aimed at identifying the key market participants (e.g., the company, customers, competitors, and collaborators) and understanding the relationships among them.

Marketing Audit: A comprehensive analysis of a company's goals and the strategy and tactics used to achieve these goals.

Marketing Mix: A cumulative description of the key components of marketing tactics: product, service, brand, price, incentives, communications, and distribution. Also referred to as Four P's: product, price, promotion, and place (see *4-P framework*).

Marketing Plan: The marketing plan is an outline of the key aspects of managing a company's offering. There is no unique "template" for writing a marketing plan; companies use diverse approaches to structure their marketing plans. Despite their differences, however, most marketing plans share many common elements such as an executive summary, a description of the company's objectives, an overview of the company's strategy, an overview of the company's marketing mix variables, an implementation plan, a set of evaluation and control benchmarks, and various background analyses that include all supporting information. This common structure is shown in Figure 4.3.

Figure 4.3. The Marketing Plan

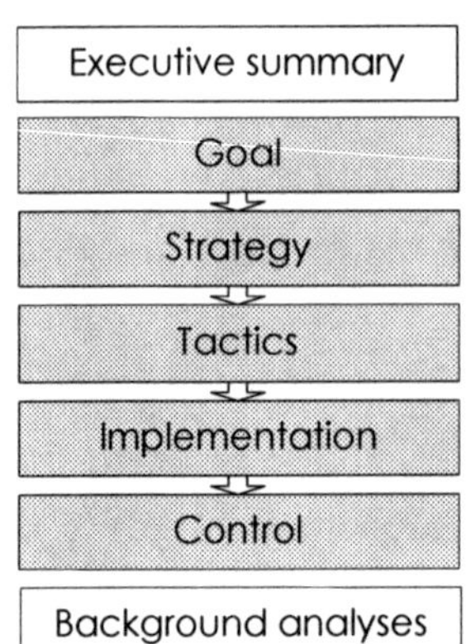

Market-Penetration Strategy: A market growth strategy aimed at increasing sales of a company's current offerings to current customers (see *product-market growth framework*).

Merchandisers: Indirect sales force that offers support to retailers for in-store activities such as shelf location, pricing, and compliance with special programs.

Multichannel Conflict: Channel conflict, which occurs when a manufacturer uses multiple channels that compete for the same customers (see also *channel conflict*).

Niche Strategy: Marketing strategy aimed at a distinct and relatively small customer segment.

Offering: The combination of marketing mix variables (product, service, image, price, incentives, communication, and distribution) that is being offered by the company to its customers. It is the product, augmented with a certain service, associated with a particular image, offered at a particular price, promoted by a particular combination of communication and sales promotion campaigns, and available through specific distribution channels.

Opportunity Analysis: Strategic process of evaluating the environment in which the company operates with the purpose of identifying opportunities for developing a new offering or optimizing existing offerings.

Opportunity Gap: A discrepancy between the company's current and potential market performance (Figure 4.4). Opportunity gap analysis is especially useful in strategic planning when a company evaluates existing market opportunities to develop a new offering.

Figure 4.4. Opportunity Gap

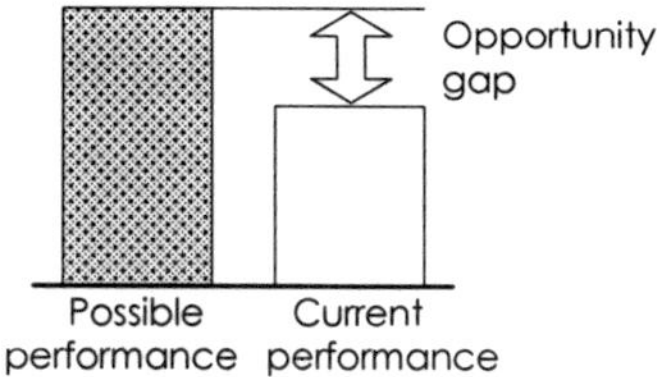

Parallel Importing: The practice of importing products from a country in which the price is lower into a country in which the same product is priced higher. A hypothetical example of this practice would be importing drugs from Canada to the United States. In most cases, parallel importing is illegal in the United States.

Pareto Principle: The 80/20 relationship discovered in the late 1800s by the economist Vilfredo Pareto.[8] Pareto established that 80% of the land in Italy was owned by 20% of the population. He later observed that 20% of the peapods in his garden yielded 80% of the peas that were harvested. The Pareto Principle, or the 80/20 Rule, has proven its validity in a number of other areas. In marketing, the most common illustration of the 80/20 rule is that 80% of revenues are likely to be generated by 20% of customers (or products).

Path of Least Resistance: Efficiency-based hierarchy of marketing strategies to increase sales. For most companies, the path of least resistance implies that it is most efficient to increase sales by starting with current customers, then by luring competitors' customers, and finally by building demand for the entire category (Figure 4.5). One exception concerns market leaders who are more likely to benefit from building category demand than from trying to steal share from a niche competitor.

Figure 4.5. The Path of Least Resistance

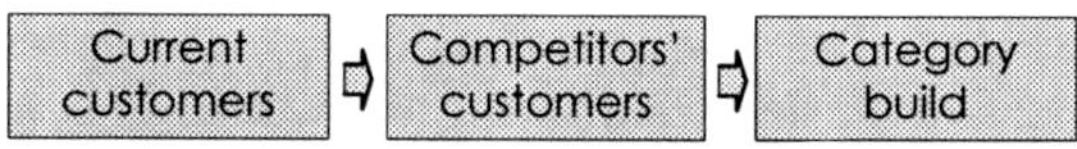

Penetration Pricing: Pricing strategy aimed at rapidly gaining market share. This strategy often leads to higher sales volume, albeit at lower margins (see also *price skimming*).

Perceptual Map: A visual representation of customer perceptions of products, services, brands, companies, etc. Typically used to display customer perceptions of competitive products (Figure 4.6).

Figure 4.6. Perceptual Map

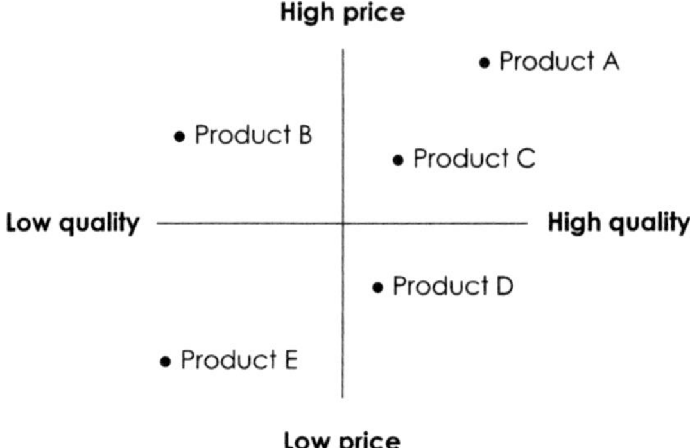

Performance Gap: A discrepancy between the desired and the actual state of affairs, between the goal and the reality (Figure 4.7). Performance gaps often include discrepancies between desired and actual gross and net revenues, profit margins, and market share.

Figure 4.7. Performance Gap

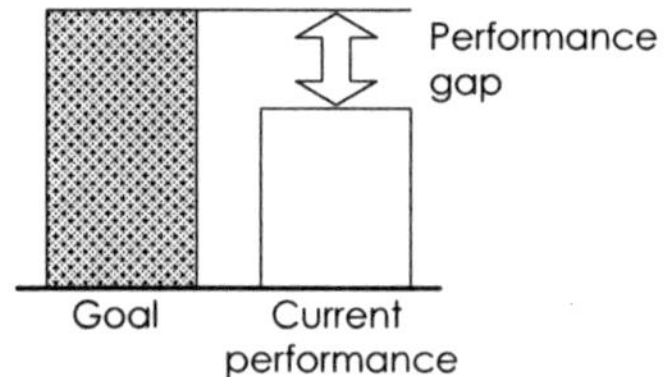

Point-of-Purchase Advertising: Promotional materials displayed at the point of purchase (e.g., in a retail store).

Portfolio Models: The main goal of the product-portfolio models is to offer direction on how to allocate resources to companies comprised of multiple strategic business units (SBUs). Two of the most popular models that came into common use in the 60s and 70s are the BSG and GE portfolio evaluation models (see *BCG and GE frameworks*).

Positioning: The process of creating a distinct image of a company's offering in a customer's mind.[9] Positioning reflects how the company wants its offering to be perceived and remembered by the customer. For example, BMW promotes its cars as being the "ultimate driving machine," Gillette razors aspire to be "the best a man can get," and Maytag's lonely repairman symbolizes reliability. Because positioning involves prioritizing an offering's existing benefits and costs in order to highlight its key distinctive benefits, the same offering can often be positioned in multiple ways.

Positioning Statement: An internal document that offers a succinct summary of the essence of a company's targeting and positioning strategy. The positioning statement is used by various divisions within the company (product development, marketing, sales force management, packaging, etc.), as well as in company communications with external agencies (advertising, public relations, distributors, etc.), to ensure that their actions are consistent with the company's strategic goal. The positioning statement has three main components: (1) target market, which identifies the customer segment targeted by the offering, (2) frame of reference, which identifies how the customer should think of the offering, and (3) unique value proposition, which identifies the reason why customers will buy the offering (also referred to as point of difference). Depending on the frame of reference, two types of positioning statements can be identified: non-comparative, which focuses on customers' needs and the ability of the target offering to deliver value to satisfy these needs without directly evoking a comparative frame (Figure 4.8) and comparative, which directly compares the company's offering to that of a competitor (Figure 4.9).

Figure 4.8. Non-Comparative Positioning Statement

.... is the best ....
(offering) (product category)

for ....
(target market)

because ....
(unique value proposition)

Figure 4.9. Comparative Positioning Statement

.... is a better ....
(offering) (product category)

than ....
(competitive offering)

for ....
(target market)

because ....
(unique value proposition)

Predatory Pricing: A strategy that involves selling below cost with the intent of driving competitors out of business. In most cases, predatory pricing is illegal in the U.S.

Prestige Pricing: Pricing strategy in which the price is set at a relatively high level for the purpose of creating an exclusive image of the offering.

Price Discrimination: A strategy that involves charging different buyers different prices for goods of equal grade and quality.

Price Fixing: Conspiracy among companies to set prices for a given product and/or service.

Price Signaling: (1) Pricing strategy that aims to capitalize on price-quality inferences (i.e., higher priced products are also likely to be higher quality). Primarily used when the actual product benefits are not readily observable (also known as *prestige pricing*). (2) Indirect communication between companies, aimed at indicating their intentions with respect to their pricing strategy.

Price Skimming: Pricing strategy whereby a new product is priced relatively high, allowing the company to maintain high margins at the expense of the volume (see also *penetration pricing*).

Private Label: Branding strategy in which an offering is branded by the retailer (e.g., Kenmore - Sear's brand for home appliances, Kirkwood – Costco's private brand). Private labels are often contrasted to national brands, which are branded by the manufacturer or a third party rather than by the retailer (e.g., Coca-Cola, IBM, Nike). Typically, private labels tend to be less expensive than the national brands although there are many exceptions such as private labels offered by upscale retailers (e.g., Marks & Spenser's clothing line).

Product Development Strategy: A market growth strategy aimed at creating new offerings for existing markets. Often done through product innovation, product augmentation, or product line extensions (see *product-market growth framework*).

Product-Line Pricing: Pricing strategy whereby the price of each individual offering is determined as a function of the offering's place in the relevant product line (e.g., the price of BMW's 3-series models is a function of the prices of its 5- and 7-series models).

Product Line Extension: see *extension.*

Product-Market Growth Matrix: A 2 (offering: existing vs. new) x 2 (market: existing vs. new) matrix advanced by Igor Ansoff[10] outlining the four key market growth strategies: *market penetration, market development, product development, and diversification* (see *product-market growth framework*).

Promotional Allowance: Trade promotion offered as a reward for conducting promotional activities on behalf of the manufacturer. Promotional allowances are typically implemented as a discount from the wholesale price rather than as a separate promotional payment. From an accounting standpoint, they are often considered as a discount to the channel rather than a marketing expense.

Psychographics: Individual differences represented by personality and lifestyle traits (e.g., activities, interests, and opinions). Most often used in segmentation and targeting decisions.

Pull Strategy: The practice of creating demand for a company's offering by promoting the offering directly to end-users, who in turn demand the offering from intermediaries, ultimately "pulling" the offering through the channel (see *push-pull framework*).

Push Strategy: The practice of creating demand for a company's offering by offering incentives to channel members, who in turn push the product downstream to end-users (see *push-pull framework*).

Reminder Advertising: Advertising strategy designed to maintain awareness and stimulate repurchase of an already established offering.

Repositioning: A change in the positioning of a given offering. The key reason for repositioning is to change the existing value proposition to better address the needs of target customers, the company, and/or its collaborators.

Reverse Engineering: The process of analyzing competitors' products (often by physically taking them apart) to learn about design characteristics, manufacturing processes, and materials.

Reverse Logistics: The process of reclaiming recyclable and reusable materials, returns, etc. for repair, remanufacturing, or disposal.

Second Market Discounting: Pricing strategy in which a company charges a lower price for the products/services it offers in more competitive markets (e.g., exports for developing countries).

Segmentation: A process of dividing buyers into groups with similar characteristics (e.g., needs, age, income, etc.) Segmentation is based on the idea that because customers in a given segment respond in a similar manner to a company's offering, they can be treated as if they were a single entity and their needs can be served by the same offering. Thus, through segmentation, the company can reduce the diversity (or heterogeneity) in the marketplace by focusing on a relatively small number of segments. Note that dividing the marketplace into separate segments is highly subjective and is likely to vary depending on the segmentation criteria. A good segmentation should yield segments that are mutually exclusive and collectively exhaustive: they should be sufficiently different from one another so that they do not overlap and, at the same time, should account for all possible outcomes.

Shrinkage: A term used by retailers to describe theft of goods by customers and employees.

Skimming: A pricing strategy in which a firm sets a high initial price in order to maximize profit margins, usually at the expense of market share.

Slotting Allowance: Incentive payment given to a retailer to allocate shelf space for a new product.

Steal-Share Strategy: Sales-volume-growth strategy aimed at a company's current customers and/or at competitors' customers rather than attracting new category users.

Strategic Business Unit (SBU): An operating company unit with a distinct set of offerings (products and/or services) sold to an identifiable group of customers, in competition with a well-defined set of competitors.

Sub-Brand: A second-tier brand name often used to mitigate the potential drawbacks of a direct brand extension, while leveraging the core brand to support the extension (e.g., Courtyard by Marriott, Ford Mustang, and Porsche Cayenne).

Supply-Chain Analysis: A method of optimizing the supply side of the manufacturing and/or service delivery process. Supply-chain analysis can be viewed as a subset of the broader concept of *value-chain analysis.*

SWOT Analysis: A popular framework focusing on four aspects of company analysis: strengths, weaknesses, opportunities, and threats.

Targeting: The process of identifying customers for whom the company and its collaborators can deliver value superior to the competition in a way that allows the company and its collaborators to achieve their strategic goals.

Trade Promotions: Promotion activities directed at channel partners such as wholesalers and retailers (rather than end-users). Typical trade promotional activities include *promotional allowances, advertising allowances,* and *cooperative advertising.*

Trademark: see intellectual property.

Two-Part Pricing: see *complementary pricing.*

Value-Chain Analysis: A method of optimizing the value-delivery process, from raw materials to the final product.

Value Curves: A method of representing an offering's performance on relevant attributes (Figure 4.10). Unlike perceptual maps which offer more holistic and usually two-dimensional representation of perceived performance, value curves are multi-dimensional and capture an offering's performance on individual attributes.

Figure 4.10. The Value Curves Method

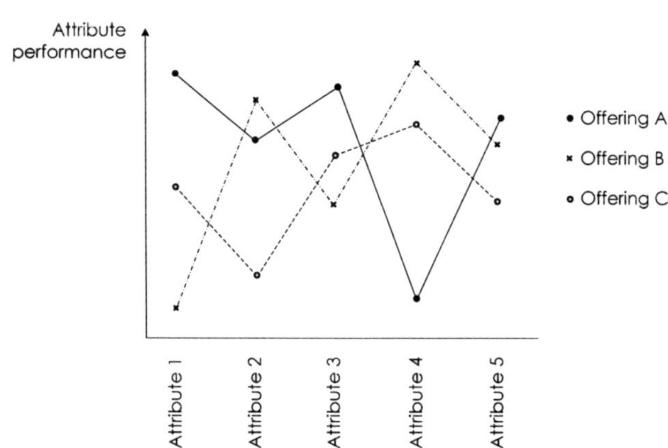

Value Equivalence Line: The value-equivalence line represents offerings for which the ratio of perceived benefits and perceived price is the same (Figure 4.11). Higher benefit, higher priced offerings are toward the upper right; lower benefit, lower priced offerings are toward the lower left.

Figure 4.11. Value Map

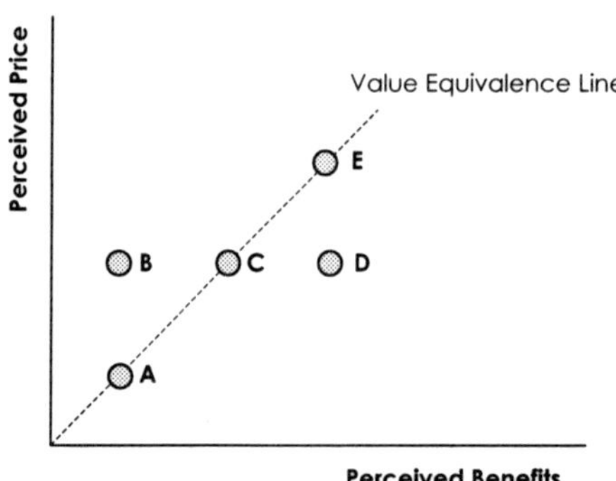

Vertical Channel Conflict occurs between different levels of the same channel (e.g., manufacturer – retailer) and is often caused by differences in their profit optimization strategies (e.g., the manufacturer prefers that the retailer carry its entire product line, whereas the retailer prefers to carry only the bestseller products from all manufacturers). See also *channel conflict.*

Vertical Extension: An extension is considered vertical if in addition to being differentiated on non-price benefits the offering is also differentiated on price (Figure 4.12). A tri-tier offering strategy built as a vertical extension is the "Good-Better-Best" strategy. To illustrate, Microsoft products: MS Suite 2002 (good), MS Office Small Business (better), and MS Office Professional (best) can be considered vertical extensions. Thus, the keyword describing many of the vertical extensions is "better" (which implies price difference in addition to the difference in benefits) rather than simply "different." Depending on the direction in which the original offering is being extended, two types of vertical extensions can be distinguished: upscale and downscale (see also *extension, horizontal extension*).

Figure 4.12. Vertical Extension

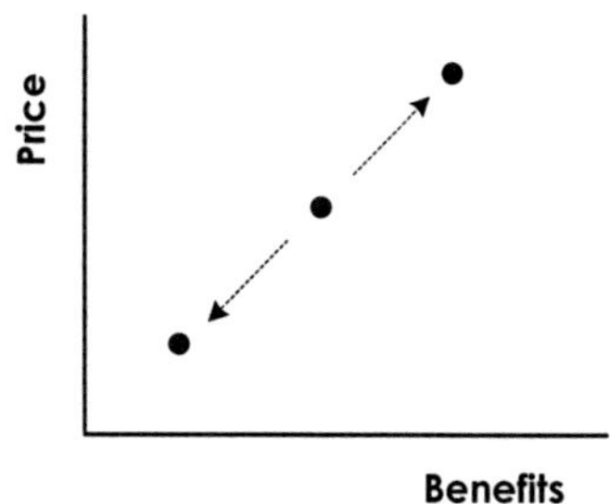

Vertical Integration: The degree of ownership within the value-delivery chain (e.g., supplier–manufacturer–distributor). Expansion of ownership upstream is referred to as backward integration, and expansion downstream is referred to as forward integration (Figure 4.13). Some of the common benefits of integration include increased control, reduced costs, optimized channel coordination and profits, and creating barriers to entry. Some of the common drawbacks include high up-front investment, potential internal inefficiencies due to lack of competition, and capacity sub-optimization resulting from fluctuations in supply and/or demand. Common alternatives to vertical integration include long-term contracts, joint ventures, and franchise agreements.

Figure 4.13. Vertical Integration Strategies

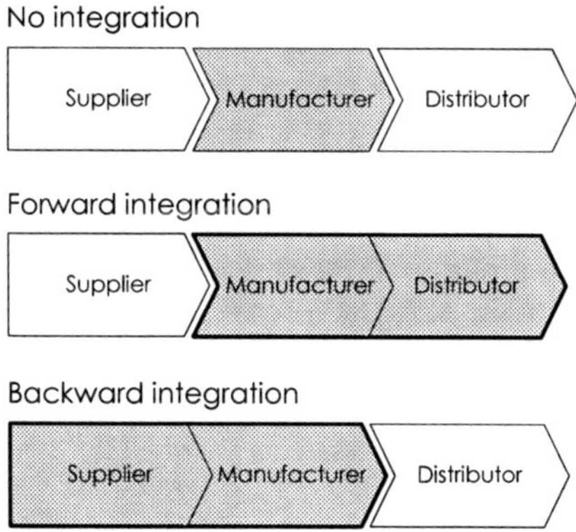

Vertical Marketing Systems: Centrally coordinated distribution channel.

Vertical Price Fixing: The (illegal) practice whereby channel partners (e.g., a manufacturer and a retailer) explicitly or implicitly collaborate to set prices (see also *horizontal price fixing*).

Volume Discount: Reduction of list price based on the quantity a buyer purchases.

Yield Management Pricing: Pricing strategy whereby price is set to maximize revenue for a set amount of capacity at a given time (typically used by airlines, hotels, etc.)

Notes

---

[1] Keller, Kevin Lane (2003), *Strategic Brand Management: Building, Measuring and Managing Brand Equity* (2nd ed.). Upper Saddle River, NJ: Prentice Hall.

[2] Ibid.

[3] Anderson, Erin, et al. (2001), *Marketing Channels* (6th ed.). Upper Saddle River, NJ: Prentice Hall.

[4] Brandenburger, Adam and Barry Nalebuff (1996), *Co-Opetition* (1st ed.). New York, NY: Doubleday.

[5] Henderson, Bruce, D. (1974), "The Experience Curve Reviewed: Why Does It Work?," in *Perspectives on Strategy: From the Boston Consulting Group* (1998), W.S. Carl and J. George Stalk, Eds. New York, NY: Wiley.

[6] Porter, Michael E. (1979), "How Competitive Forces Shape Strategy," Harvard Business Review, 57, 137-145.

[7] Henderson, Bruce, D. (1973), "The Experience Curve Reviewed: History," in *Perspectives on Strategy: From the Boston Consulting Group* (1998), W.S. Carl and J. George Stalk, Eds. New York, NY: Wiley.

[8] Koch, Richard (1998), *The 80/20 Principle: The Secret to Success by Achieving More with Less.* New York, NY: Doubleday.

[9] Ries, Al and Jack Trout (2001), *Positioning: The Battle for Your Mind* (20th anniversary ed.). New York, NY: McGraw-Hill.

[10] Ansoff, H. Igor (1979), *Strategic Management.* New York, NY: Wiley.

4.2. Key Financial Concepts

Break-Even Analysis: Analysis aimed at identifying the break-even point at which the benefits and costs associated with a particular action are equal and beyond which profit occurs. The four most common types of break-even analyses are: (1) *break-even of a fixed-cost investment*, (2) *break-even of a price cut*, (3) *break-even of a variable-cost increase*, and (4) *cannibalization break-even analysis.*

Break-Even Analysis of a Fixed-Cost Investment: Fixed-cost break-even analysis identifies the sales volume at which a company neither makes a profit nor incurs a loss after making a fixed-cost investment (see Appendix 2 for more details).

Break-Even Analysis of a Price Cut: Break-even rate of a price cut identifies the increase in the sales volume that needs to be achieved in order for the price cut to have no impact on profitability (see Appendix 3 for more details).

Break-Even Analysis of a Variable-Cost Increase: Break-even analysis of a variable-cost increase identifies the increase in the sales volume that needs to be achieved in order for the increase in variable costs to have no impact on profitability (see Appendix 4 for more details).

Break-Even Analysis of Cannibalization: Break-even analysis of cannibalization identifies the ratio of the cannibalized sales volume of an existing offering to the sales volume generated by a new offering at which a company neither makes a profit nor incurs a loss.

Contribution: Contribution is the difference between gross revenues and total variable costs. Contribution can also be calculated on a per-unit basis as the difference between unit selling price and unit variable cost (i.e., the dollar amount that each unit sold "contributes" to the payment of fixed costs).

$$\text{Contribution}_{(\text{Total})} = \text{Gross revenue} - \text{Variable costs}_{(\text{Total})}$$

$$\text{Contribution}_{(\text{Unit})} = \text{Price}_{(\text{Unit})} - \text{Variable costs}_{(\text{Unit})}$$

Contribution Margin: Contribution margin is the ratio of total *contribution* to total revenues. Contribution margin also can be expressed as the ratio of unit contribution to unit's selling price.

$$\text{Contribution margin} = \frac{\text{Contribution}_{(\text{Total})}}{\text{Gross revenue}} = \frac{\text{Contribution}_{(\text{Unit})}}{\text{Price}_{(\text{Unit})}}$$

Conversion Rate: The number of potential customers who have tried the product/service relative to the total number of customers aware of the product/service.

$$\text{Conversion rate} = \frac{\text{Current and former customers}}{\text{Potential customers aware of the offering}}$$

Cost of Goods Sold (COGS): Expenses directly related to creating the goods or services being sold. Cost of goods sold can have a *variable* (e.g., the cost of raw materials, the cost of turning raw materials into goods) and a *fixed* component (e.g., depreciation of equipment).

Cost Per Point (CPP): Measure used to represent the cost of a communications campaign. CPP is the media cost of reaching one percent (one rating point) of a particular demographic.

$$\text{CPP} = \frac{\text{Advertising cost}}{\text{GRP}}$$

Cost Per Thousand (CPM): Measure used to represent the cost of a communications campaign. CPM is the cost of reaching 1,000 individuals or households with an advertising message in a given medium (M is the Roman numeral for 1,000). For example, a TV commercial that costs $200,000 to air and reaches 10M viewers has a CPM of $20. The popularity of CPM derives in part from its being a good comparative measure of advertising efficiency across different media (e.g., TV, print, Internet).

$$\text{CPM} = \frac{\text{Advertising cost}}{\text{Total impressions}} \cdot 1{,}000$$

Cross-Elasticity of Demand: The percentage change in quantity sold of a given offering caused by a percentage change in a marketing variable for another offering (e.g., advertising, sales promotions, price).

Cross-Price Elasticity: The percentage change in quantity sold of a given offering caused by a percentage change in the price of another offering.

Fixed Costs: Fixed costs are expenses that do not fluctuate with output volume within a relevant time period (see Appendix 1 for more details).

Frequency: The number of times the target audience is exposed to an advertisement in a given period of time. Also used in reference to the number of times an advertisement is repeated through a specific medium over a specific time period.

Goodwill: Accounting term referring to a company's intangible assets. Goodwill is recorded on a company's books when it acquires another company, and pays a premium over the listed book value of its assets. The excess paid is categorized as goodwill, added to the acquiring company's balance sheet as an asset, and then depreciated over time (usually 15 years). The Internal Revenue Code defines goodwill as the value of a trade or business attributable to the expectancy of continued customer patronage. Such value results from several factors, including quality product lines and stable employees.

Gross (Profit) Margin: Gross margin is the ratio of *gross profit* to gross revenues (sometimes also used as a synonym for gross profit). Gross margin analysis is a useful tool because it implicitly includes unit-selling prices of products or services, unit costs, and unit volume. Note, however, the difference between *gross margin* and *contribution margin*: Gross margin includes some, but often not all, *variable costs,* some of which can be part of the *operating margin.*

$$\text{Gross margin} = \frac{\text{Gross profit}}{\text{Gross revenue}} = \frac{\text{Gross revenue - Cost of goods sold}}{\text{Gross revenue}}$$

Gross Profit: Gross profit is the difference between total sales revenue and total cost of goods sold. Gross profit can be also calculated on a per-unit basis as the difference between unit selling price and unit cost of goods sold. To illustrate, if a company sells 100 units each priced at $1 and each costing the company $.30 to manufacture, then the unit gross profit is $.70, the total gross profit is $70, and the unit and total gross margins are 70%.

$$\text{Gross profit}_{(\text{Total})} = \text{Gross revenues}_{(\text{Total})} - \text{Cost of goods sold}_{(\text{Total})}$$

$$\text{Gross profit}_{(\text{Unit})} = \text{Price}_{(\text{Unit})} - \text{Cost of goods sold}_{(\text{Unit})}$$

Gross Rating Point (GRP): A measure of the total volume of advertising delivery to the target audience. It is equal to the percent of population reached times the frequency of exposure. To illustrate, if a given advertisement reaches 60% of the households with an average frequency of 3 times, then the GRP of the media is equal to 180. GRP can also be calculated by dividing the gross impressions by the size of the total audience. A single GRP represents 1% of the total audience in a given region.

$$\text{GRP} = \text{Reach} \cdot \text{Frequency}$$

Income Statement: Financial document showing a company's income and expenses over a given period (see Appendix 5).

Marginal Cost: The cost of producing one extra unit.

Market Share: A brand's share of the total sales of all offerings within the product category in which the brand competes. Market share is determined by dividing a brand's sales volume by the total category sales volume, where sales can be defined in terms of revenues or on a unit basis (e.g., number of items sold or number of customers served).

$$\text{Market share} = \frac{\text{An offering's sales in market X}}{\text{Total sales in market X}}$$

Market Size: Monetary value of an existing or potential market, typically on an annual basis. Market size is also used in reference to the number of customers comprising a particular market.

$$\text{Market size} = \text{Number of customers} \cdot \text{Annual volume purchased} \cdot \text{Purchase price}$$

Mark-up: see *trade margin.*

Net Earnings: see *net income.*

Net Income: *Gross revenues* minus all costs and expenses (e.g., cost of goods sold, operating expenses, depreciation, interest, and taxes) in a given period of time.

$$\text{Net income} = \text{Gross revenues} - \text{Total costs}$$

Net Margin: Net margin is the ratio of *net income* to gross revenues.

$$\text{Net margin} = \frac{\text{Net income}}{\text{Gross revenues}}$$

Operating Expenses: The primary costs, other than cost of goods sold, incurred in order to generate revenues (e.g., sales, marketing, R&D, general and administrative expenses).

Operating Income: *Gross profit* minus *operating expenses.* Operating income reflects the firm's profitability from current operations without regard to the interest charges accruing from the capital structure.

$$\text{Operating income} = \text{Gross profit} - \text{Operating expenses}$$

Operating Margin: Operating margin is the ratio of *operating income* to gross revenues.

$$\text{Operating margin} = \frac{\text{Operating income}}{\text{Gross revenues}}$$

Penetration Rate: The number of customers who have tried the offering at least once relative to the total number of potential customers.

$$\text{Penetration rate} = \frac{\text{Current and former customers}}{\text{Potential customers}}$$

Price Elasticity: A variable representing the percentage change in quantity sold relative to the percentage change in price for a given product or service. Because the quantity demanded decreases when the price increases, this ratio is negative; however, for practical purposes, the absolute value of the ratio is taken, and price elasticity is often reported as a positive number. To illustrate, price elasticity of -2 means that a 5% price increase will result in a 10% decrease in the quantity sold. In cases where price elasticity is greater than one ($|E_p| > 1$), the demand is said to be elastic in the sense that a change in price will cause an even larger change in quantity demanded. In contrast, when price elasticity is less than one ($|E_p| < 1$), the demand is said to be inelastic, meaning that a change in price will result in a smaller change in quantity demanded. When price elasticity is equal to one ($|E_p| = 1$), the demand is said to be unitary, meaning that a change in price will result in an equal change in quantity demanded. Note that because it reflects proportional changes, price elasticity does not depend on the units in which the price and quantity are expressed. Note also that because price elasticity is a function of the initial values, the same absolute changes in price can lead to different price elasticity values. To illustrate, the impact of lowering the price by 5 cents will vary based on the initial price: it is 5% of an initial price of $1.00 but only 1% of an initial price of $5.00.

$$E_p = \frac{\Delta Q\%}{\Delta P\%} = \frac{\Delta Q \cdot P}{\Delta P \cdot Q}$$

Reach: The size of the audience that has been exposed to a particular advertisement at least once in a given time period (multiple viewings by the same audience do not increase reach). For example, if 40,000 of 100,000 different households were exposed to a given commercial at least once, the reach is 40%. Reach may be stated either as an absolute number or as a fraction of a population.

Retention Rate: The number of customers who have repurchased the offering during the current buying cycle (e.g., month, quarter, year) relative to the number of customers who have purchased the offering during the last cycle. Also used in reference to the number of customers who have repurchased the offering relative to the total number of customers who have tried the product at least once.

$$\text{Retention rate} = \frac{\text{Active customers during the current period}}{\text{Active customers during the last period}}$$

Target Rating Point (TRP): A measure of the total volume of advertising delivery to the target audience. TRP is similar to GRP, but its calculation involves using only the target audience (rather than the total audience watching the program) as the base. Thus, a single TRP represents 1% of the targeted viewers in any particular region. Many advertising agencies use TRP and GRP interchangeably.

Total Costs: The sum of the fixed and variable costs (see Appendix 1 for more details).

Trade Margin: Trade margin is the difference between unit selling price and unit cost at each level of a marketing channel (see Appendix 6). A trade margin is frequently referred to as a markup by channel members and is often expressed as a percentage. Trade margins are typically determined on the basis of selling price, but practices vary among firms and industries.

Variable Costs: Variable costs are expenses that fluctuate in direct proportion to the output volume of units produced (see Appendix 1 for more details).

Variable Margin: The ratio of *variable profit* to *gross revenues*.

Variable Profit: *Gross revenues* minus *variable costs*.

Appendix 1: Fixed, Variable, and Total Costs

Cost accounting identifies three basic types of costs: fixed costs, variable costs, and total costs. These three cost types are outlined in more detail below.

Fixed costs are expenses that do not fluctuate with output volume within a relevant time period. Typical examples of fixed costs include research and development expenses, rent, interest on debt, insurance, plant and equipment expenses, and salary of permanent full-time workers. Note that even though their absolute size remains unchanged regardless of the output volume, fixed costs become progressively smaller per unit of output as volume increases, a decrease that results from the larger number of output units over which fixed costs are allocated.

In contrast, *variable costs* are expenses that fluctuate in direct proportion to the output volume of units produced. To illustrate, communication-related expenses (e.g., advertising and public relations) typically do not depend on the number of units sold and, therefore, are likely to be considered fixed marketing costs, whereas expenses incurred by consumer incentives (e.g., coupons, price discounts, and rebates) are commonly viewed as variable marketing costs. Other expenses such as channel incentives (e.g., promotional allowances) and sales force compensation can be classified either as fixed or variable costs depending on their structure (e.g., performance-based compensation vs. fixed salary).

Finally, the term *total costs* refers to the sum of the fixed and variable costs. The relationship between fixed, variable, and total costs can be illustrated as shown in Figure 1.

It is important to note that deciding which costs are fixed and which costs are variable depends on the time horizon. To illustrate, in the short run, the salaries of permanent full-time employees will be considered as fixed costs because they do not depend on the output volume. In the longer run, however, a company might adjust the number and/or the salaries of the permanent employees based on the demand for its products or services – a scenario in which these costs would be considered variable rather than fixed. Thus, in the long run all costs would be considered variable.

Figure 1: The Relationship between Fixed, Variable, and Total Costs

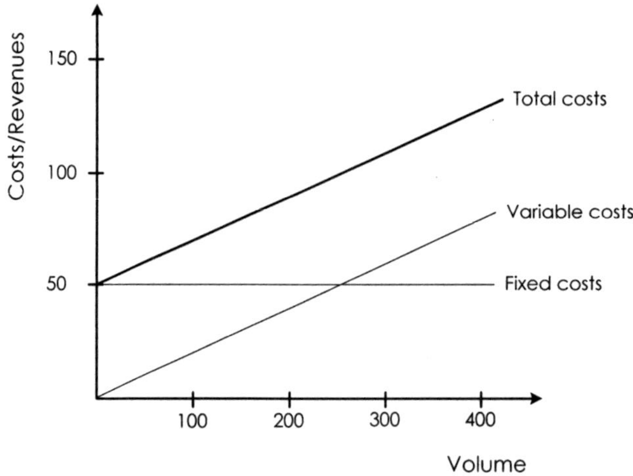

Appendix 2: Break-Even Analysis of a Fixed Cost Investment

Break-even analysis of a fixed-cost investment identifies the unit or dollar sales volume at which the company is able to recoup a particular investment such as research and development expenses, product improvement costs, and/or the costs of an advertising campaign. The break-even volume of a fixed-cost investment (BEV_{FC}) is the ratio of the size of the fixed-cost investment to the unit margin (also referred to as contribution per unit).

$$BEV_{FC} = \frac{\text{Fixed-cost investment}}{\text{Unit margin}}$$

Because the unit margin can be expressed as the difference between the unit selling price and unit variable costs, the break-even volume is also often given as:

$$BEV_{FC} = \frac{\text{Fixed-cost investment}}{\text{Unit selling price - Unit variable cost}}$$

The break-even analysis of a fixed cost investment can be illustrated as shown in Figure 2.

Figure 2: Break-Even of a Fixed Cost Investment

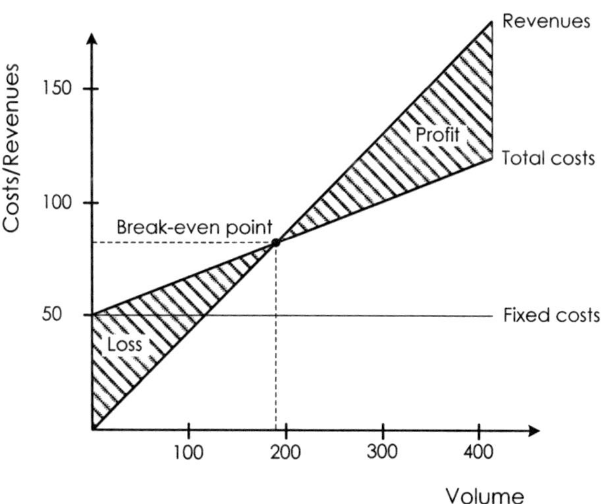

To illustrate, consider an offering priced at $100 with variable costs of $50 and fixed costs of $50M. In this case,

$$BEV_{FC} = \frac{\text{Fixed-cost investment}}{\text{Unit margin}} = \frac{\$50M}{\$100\text{-}\$50} = 1{,}000{,}000$$

This implies that in order for the $50M fixed-cost investment to break even, the sales volume should reach 1,000,000 items.

In addition to the break-even analysis of a fixed cost investment associated with launching a new offering, a company might need to calculate the break-even volume of a change (most often an increase) in its current fixed-cost investment. Typical problems to which this type of analysis could be applied are estimating the incremental increase in sales necessary to cover the costs of an R&D project, the costs of an advertising campaign, and even the costs of increasing the compensation package of senior executives. The break-even analysis of such increase in the fixed-cost investment is shown in Figure 3.

Figure 3: Break-Even of an Increase in the Fixed-Cost Investment

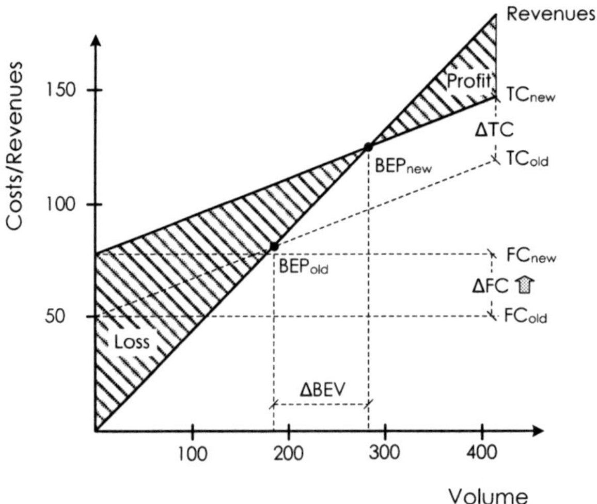

To illustrate, consider the impact of an increase in the fixed costs from $50M to $60M for a product priced at $100 with variable costs of $50. In this case,

$$BEV_{FC} = \frac{\text{Fixed-cost investment}}{\text{Unit margin}} = \frac{\$60M\text{-}\$50M}{\$100\text{-}\$50} = 200{,}000$$

This implies that in order for the $10M fixed-cost investment to break even, the sales volume should increase by 200,000 items.

Appendix 3: Break-Even Analysis of a Price Cut

The impact of a price cut on profitability is twofold. On one hand, lowering the price tends to increase the unit volume sold, thus increasing total revenues. On the other hand, lowering the price decreases the unit contribution margin, thus lowering total revenues. In this context, break-even analysis estimates the increase in sales volume that needs to be achieved in order for the price cut to have neutral impact on profitability. The break-even analysis of a price cut is shown in Figure 4.

Figure 4: Break-Even of a Decrease in Revenues (Due to a Price Cut)

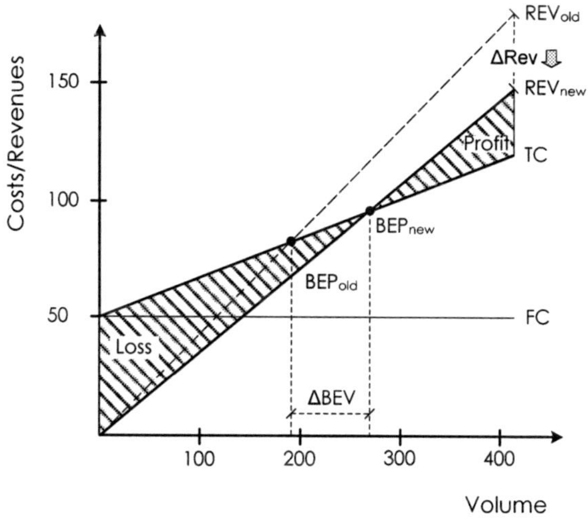

To break even, lost profits because of the lower margin resulting from the price cut must be equal to the additional profits generated from the incremental volume due to low price. Thus, to have a neutral or positive impact on the company's bottom line, the additional profits generated from the incremental volume resulting from the low price must be equal or greater than the lost profits that result from the lower contribution margin.

$$\text{Profit}_{\text{NewPrice}} \geq \text{Profit}_{\text{OldPrice}} \quad (1)$$

Given that profit is a function of volume and margins, the above equation can be modified as follows:

$$\text{Volume}_{\text{NewPrice}} \cdot \text{Margin}_{\text{NewPrice}} \geq \text{Volume}_{\text{OldPrice}} \cdot \text{Margin}_{\text{OldPrice}} \quad (2)$$

Now, the above equation can be restructured as follows:

$$Volume_{NewPrice} \geq \frac{Margin_{OldPrice}}{Margin_{NewPrice}} \cdot Volume_{OldPrice} \quad (3)$$

Hence, the sales volume that needs to be achieved for a price cut to break even is:

$$BEV_{PC} = \frac{Margin_{OldPrice}}{Margin_{NewPrice}} \cdot Volume_{OldPrice} \quad (4)$$

In addition to calculating the break-even volume of a price cut, it might be useful to calculate the rate at which the sales volume must increase in order for the price cut to be profitable. In this context, the break-even rate of a price cut (BER_{PC}) can be derived from equation (2) as follows:

$$\frac{Volume_{NewPrice}}{Volume_{OldPrice}} \geq \frac{Margin_{OldPrice}}{Margin_{NewPrice}} \quad (5)$$

$$\frac{Volume_{NewPrice}}{Volume_{OldPrice}} - 1 \geq \frac{Margin_{OldPrice}}{Margin_{NewPrice}} - 1 \quad (6)$$

$$\frac{Volume_{NewPrice} - Volume_{OldPrice}}{Volume_{OldPrice}} \geq \frac{Margin_{OldPrice}}{Margin_{NewPrice}} - 1 \quad (7)$$

Note that the right side of the equation reflects the increase in volume resulting from the price cut as a percentage of the initial volume before the price cut. Hence, the Break-Even Rate (BER_{PC}) at which the sales should increase so that the price cut has neutral impact on profitability is:

$$BER_{PC} = \frac{Margin_{OldPrice}}{Margin_{NewPrice}} - 1 \quad (8)$$

To illustrate, consider the impact of a price cut from \$100 to \$75 for a product with variable cost of \$50. In this case, $Margin_{OldPrice}$ = \$100 - \$50 = \$50 and $Margin_{NewPrice}$ = \$100 - \$75 = \$25. Therefore, the break-even volume can be calculated as follows:

$$BEV_{PC} = \frac{Margin_{OldPrice}}{Margin_{NewPrice}} \cdot Volume_{OldPrice} = \frac{\$50}{\$25} \cdot Volume_{OldPrice} = 2 \cdot Volume_{OldPrice}$$

This essentially means that in order for the price cut to break even, the sales volume should double at the lower price. It is noteworthy that relatively small changes in the sales price could require what might appear to be a disproportionately greater in-

crease in sales volume. Indeed, in our case a 25% decrease in price requires doubling the sales volume.
Alternatively, one could calculate the rate at which the current volume should increase so that the price cut has neutral impact on profitability.

$$BER_{PC} = \frac{Margin_{OldPrice}}{Margin_{NewPrice}} - 1 = \frac{\$50}{\$25} - 1 = 1$$

The above calculation means that in order for the price cut to break even, the sales volume should increase by a factor of 1, or by 100%.

Appendix 4: Break-Even Analysis of a Variable-Cost Increase

Break-even analysis of a variable-cost increase identifies the sales volume at which a company neither makes a profit nor incurs a loss after increasing the variable costs associated with a particular offering. Typical problems to which this type of analysis could be applied are estimating the incremental increase in sales necessary to cover an increase in the cost of goods sold, the costs associated with increasing the item-specific level of service, and the costs associated with running item-specific incentives (e.g., premiums). The break-even analysis of a variable-cost increase is shown in Figure 5.

Figure 5: Break-Even of a Variable-Cost Increase

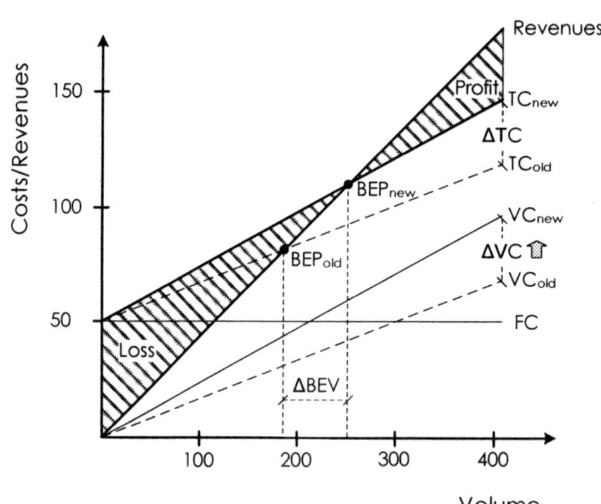

The basic principle of calculating the break-even point of an increase in an offering's variable costs is similar to that of estimating the break-even point of a price cut, with the key difference that in this case the decrease in the profit margin generated by the new offering is a result of an increase in the offering's costs rather than a decrease in revenues. Thus, the break-even volume of a variable-cost increase can be calculated as follows:

$$BEV_{VC} = \frac{\text{Margin}_{OldVC}}{\text{Margin}_{NewVC}} \cdot \text{Volume}_{OldVC}$$

Similarly, the break-even rate of an increase in the variable costs can be calculated as follows:

$$BER_{VC} = \frac{Margin_{OldVC}}{Margin_{NewVC}} - 1$$

To illustrate, consider the impact of an increase in variable costs from \$50 to \$60 for a product priced at \$100. In this case, $Margin_{OldVC}$ = \$100 - \$50 = \$50 and $Margin_{NewVC}$ = \$100 - \$60 = \$40. Therefore, the break-even volume of a variable-cost increase can be calculated as follows:

$$BEV_{VC} = \frac{Margin_{OldVC}}{Margin_{NewVC}} \cdot Volume_{OldVC} = \frac{\$50}{\$40} \cdot Volume_{OldVC} = 1.25 \cdot Volume_{OldVC}$$

This means that in order for the variable-cost increase to break even, the sales volume should increase by a factor of 1.25 or by 125%.

Alternatively, one could calculate the rate at which the current volume should increase so that the increase in variable costs has neutral impact on profitability.

$$BER_{VC} = \frac{Margin_{OldVC}}{Margin_{NewVC}} - 1 = \frac{\$50}{\$40} - 1 = 0.25$$

The above calculation implies that in order for the increase in variable costs to break even, the sales volume should increase by a factor of .25, or by 25%.

Appendix 5: An Example of Revenues, Costs, and Margins as Shown in a Company's Income Statement

Gross Revenues	
Product sales	$ 12,000
Services	3,000
Total Revenues	15,000
Cost of Goods Sold	
Product costs	4,000
Services costs	1,500
Depreciation	500
Total Cost of Goods Sold	6,000
Gross Profit	9,000
Gross Margin	60%
Operating Expenses	
Sales and Marketing	5,000
General and Administrative	1,000
Research and Development	1,500
Total Operating Expenses	7,500
Operating Income	1,500
Operating Margin	10%
Interest payments on loans	500
Earnings before taxes	1,000
Provision for taxes	250
Earnings (Net Income)	750
Profit Margin	5%

Appendix 6: An Example of Distribution Margin Analysis

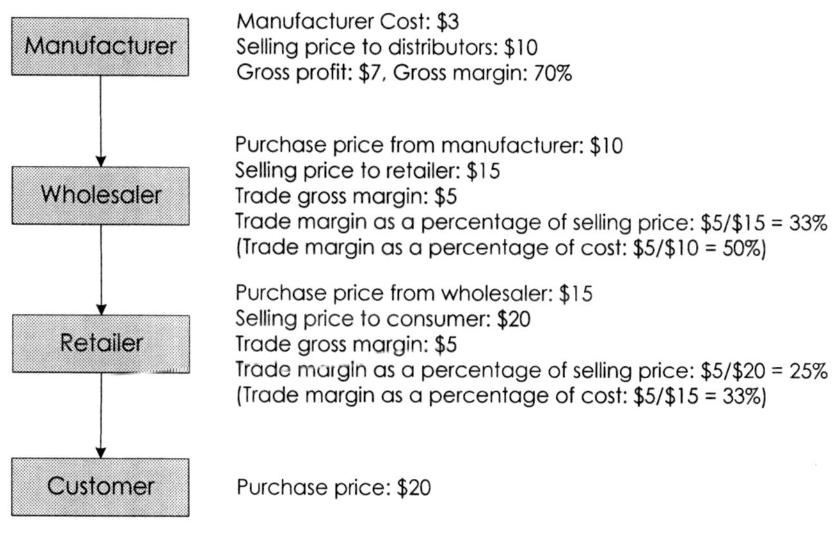

Note that margins are almost universally calculated based on the sales revenue (e.g., sales price) rather than based on the cost (e.g., purchase price). To illustrate, the margin for an item purchased for $10 (cost) and sold for $15 (revenue) can be calculated as follows:

$$\text{Margin} = \frac{\text{Revenue - Cost}}{\text{Revenue}} = \frac{\text{Selling price - Purchase price}}{\text{Selling price}} = \frac{\$15 - \$10}{\$15} = 0.33$$

Chapter 5: Frameworks

5.1. Overview

Frameworks are the cornerstones of business analysis because they offer a simplified description of complex processes and provide a general solution to a variety of industry-specific problems. Frameworks streamline the decision process by providing managers with a common view on how to frame the problem, with a universal approach to identifying alternative solutions and a shared vocabulary to discuss the issues. Because of their level of generality, frameworks rarely offer solutions to specific business problems. Instead, they provide a general algorithm which, when applied to a specific scenario, allows managers to identify the optimal solution.

Based on their level of generality, three types of business frameworks can be distinguished: meta-frameworks, strategic frameworks, and tactical frameworks.

- *Meta-frameworks* are very general frameworks that offer an overarching perspective on how to approach business problems. Because of their level of generality, meta-frameworks typically incorporate several more specific frameworks.
- *Strategic frameworks* provide a logical structure for developing and managing a company's strategic decisions, such as evaluating the competitive environment, selecting target markets, and developing a sustainable value proposition.
- *Tactical frameworks* offer a systematic approach for developing and evaluating the tactical aspects of the company's activities, such as decisions concerning various marketing mix variables (product, service, brand, price, incentives, communications, and distribution).

These three types of frameworks vary in terms of their level of abstraction; meta-frameworks are the most abstract, whereas tactical frameworks are the most concrete. The relationship between these three types of frameworks is illustrated in Figure 5.1.

Figure 5.1. Framework Types

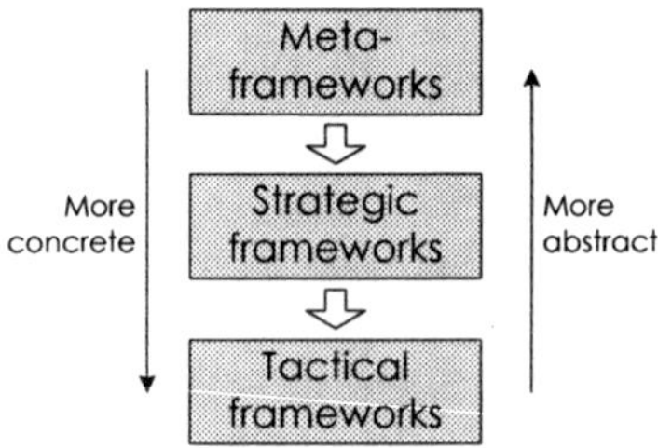

Meta-Frameworks for Case Analysis

Meta-frameworks describe generic methods for making business decisions and are used as overarching frameworks to incorporate other, more specific frameworks. This book introduced two key meta-frameworks for analyzing and solving business cases.

- **The G-S-T-I-C Framework**
  The Goal-Strategy-Tactics-Implementation-Control (G-S-T-I-C) framework is a relatively simple and very useful approach for solving planning cases involving the formulation and/or implementation of a new business program.
- **The P-C-S Framework**
  The Problem-Cause-Solution (P-C-S) framework is a relatively simple and very useful approach for solving performance-gap cases. Unlike the G-S-T-I-C framework in which the primary focus is on formulating and implementing a new business program, the P-C-S framework is focused on identifying and rectifying problems in an existing program. The P-C-S analysis involves three key steps: formulating the problem, identifying its primary actionable cause, and developing a solution that eliminates the cause, thus solving the problem.

Strategic Frameworks for Case Analysis

Strategic frameworks deal with issues involving a company's strategy, such as market structure (customers, company, collaborators, competitors, and context) and marketing value (customer value, company value, and collaborator value). This book introduced a number of frameworks that represent some of the most popular approaches used for analyzing and solving strategic problems. A list of the key frameworks described so far in this book is given below.

- **The Goal Analysis Framework**
  The goal-analysis framework is a decision tree approach for identifying the hierarchical structure of a company's goals.
- **The 5-C Framework**
  The 5-C framework (customers, company, collaborators, competitors, and context) offers a systematic approach to evaluating the market environment.
- **The Marketing Value (3-V) Framework**
  The marketing value framework (company value, customer value, and collaborator value) is used to optimize the value of the offering to relevant market participants.
- **The Share-Market Growth Framework**
  The share-market growth framework is a method for evaluating a company's growth potential in the context of share-growth versus market-growth strategies.
- **The Product-Market Growth Framework**
  The product-market growth framework (also referred to as the Ansoff matrix) is a method for evaluating a company's expansion prospects and for developing sales-growth strategies.
- **The SWOT Framework**
  The SWOT framework uses a systematic approach to analyzing a company's overall business condition by evaluating its strengths, weaknesses, opportunities, and threats.
- **The Five Forces Framework**
  The five forces framework is a method for conducting industry analysis, making decisions concerning entering and/or exiting an industry, and evaluating the competitive aspects of a company's offering.

In addition to the frameworks explicitly addressed in the previous discussion, there are several additional frameworks that merit attention. A brief summary of five such frameworks is given below and is followed by a more detailed overview of each individual framework.

- **The 3-C Framework**
  The 3-C framework (customers, company, and competitors) offers a systematic approach to evaluating the market environment.
- **The Value-Chain Framework**
  The value-chain framework (supplier, manufacturer, channel,

customer) is a systematic approach to examining an organization's value-delivery process.

- **The S-T-P Framework**
  The S-T-P framework is a method for identifying target segments and developing segment-specific communication strategies.
- **The 7-S Framework**
  The 7-S framework offers a systematic approach to analyzing the effectiveness of an organization by evaluating its seven key characteristics: strategy, skills, shared values, structure, staff, systems, and style.
- **The BCG Product-Portfolio Framework**
  The BCG product-portfolio framework (also referred to as the BCG matrix) is a method for evaluating the overall performance of a company's strategic business units and for making cash-allocation recommendations.
- **The GE Product-Portfolio Framework**
  The GE product-portfolio framework (also referred to as the GE-McKinsey matrix) is a comprehensive method for evaluating the overall performance of a company's strategic business units and making cash-allocation recommendations.

Tactical Frameworks for Case Analysis

Tactical frameworks deal with issues involving a company's tactics, such as the processes of creating, communicating, and delivering value. In addition to the marketing mix framework outlined earlier in this book, there are several tactical frameworks that might be relevant in case analysis. A brief summary of some of the key tactical frameworks is outlined below and is followed by a more detailed overview of each individual framework.

- **The C-C-D Marketing Mix Framework**
  The C-C-D marketing mix framework (creating value, communicating value, delivering value) is a particularly useful framework for analyzing the tactical aspect of an offering.
- **The 4-P Framework**
  The 4-P framework (product, price, promotion, and place) is used to analyze the tactical aspect of an offering.
- **Product Life Cycle Framework**
  The product life cycle model offers a better understanding of

the four distinct stages in the life cycle of a product: introduction, growth, maturity, and decline.

- **A-T-R Product Adoption Framework**
  The A-T-R model identifies the key stages of the product adoption process by an individual consumer.
- **Push-Pull Promotions Framework**
  The push-pull model is a useful tool for understanding and optimizing the effectiveness of promotional resources.
- **A-I-D-A Communications Framework**
  The A-I-D-A model offers a practical approach to planning advertising activities by linking them to four key consumer decision processes: attention, interest, desire, and action.

5.2. The 3-C Framework

Snapshot: Company, competition, customer

Overview: The 3-C model, advanced by Kenichi Ohmae, suggests that a strategist should focus on three key factors for success: (1) the corporation, (2) the customer, and (3) the competition (Figure 5.2).[1] By understanding these three factors and integrating them into a strategic framework (or, to use Ohmae's terminology, a strategic triangle), the company can achieve a sustainable competitive advantage. The corporation's goal is to deliver superior value to its customers, relative to the competition, which, according to Ohmae, results from the corporation's competitive cost advantage. Applied to marketing, the 3-C framework suggests that managers need to evaluate the marketing environment in which they operate: the strengths and weaknesses of their own company, the needs of their customers, and the strengths and weaknesses of their competitors. The 3-C framework is simple, intuitive, and easy to understand and use – factors that have contributed to its popularity.

Figure 5.2. The 3-C Framework[2]

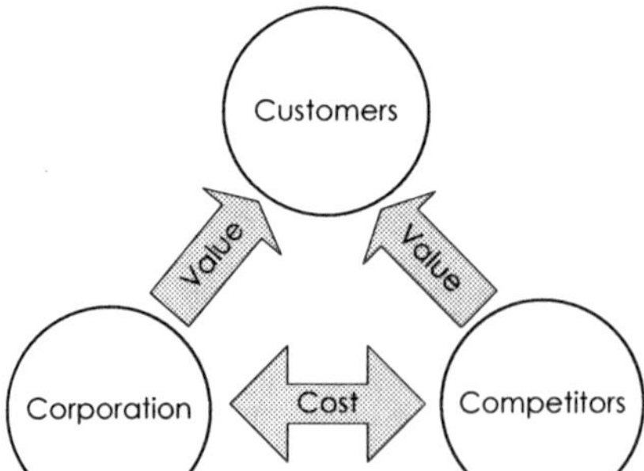

Common Misconceptions: One of the most common misinterpretations of the 3-C framework occurs when unrelated factors also starting with "c," such as capacity and cost,[3] are included as a part of the 3-C model. Recall that the C's describe the main players in the marketplace (i.e., company, customers, and competitors). Capacity and cost, on the other hand, are characteristics of the company and are not participants in the marketing exchange. Note that the issue here is not whether cost and capacity are important factors in marketing analysis but whether they conform to the logic used to identify the C's as the main factors that need to be taken into account when designing a company's business strategy.[4] The same logic applies to other potential C's such as category, complexity, core competencies, and creativity.

Limitations: An important limitation of the 3-C framework is that it does not explicitly account for a number of important environmental factors. To illustrate, a company's collaborators are not part of the 3-C model, despite the important role collaborators (e.g., suppliers and distributors) play in developing and delivering a company's offerings. Another limitation of the 3-C framework is that it does not explicitly account for the variety of economic, regulatory, technological, and political factors that comprise the context in which the company operates.

Reconceptualization: The 5-C Framework extends the 3-C framework to add collaborators and context as key strategic factors in analyzing the market structure. The inclusion of collaborators is a reflection of the important role a company's collaborators (e.g., suppliers and distributors) play in the process of creating, communicating, and delivering value to target customers. In fact, many successful offerings such as Apache web server software, Linux operating system, Mozilla Firefox Internet browser, and Wikipedia, the user-contributed online encyclopedia, are based entirely on collaboration.

Figure 5.3. The 3-C Framework[5]

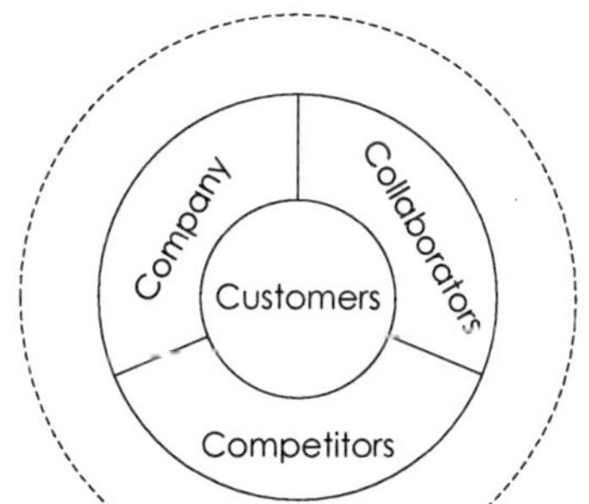

In the same vein, including the context as a key market factor is a reflection of the importance of the variety of economic, regulatory, technological, and political factors that could influence the value of the offering to target customers. Another important advantage of the 5-C Framework is that its visual representation, shown in Figure 5.3, reflects the nature of the relationships between the key market factors, and, in particular, the fact that the marketplace is defined by a specific customer need and the company's collaborators and competitors are defined relative to this need..

Application: The 3-C framework offers a simple approach for categorizing different aspects of the marketing environment and introduces a simple structure for evaluating various business problems. However, because it excludes important market and environmental factors (i.e., collaborator and context), business analysis can be better served by the more comprehensive 5-C framework discussed in an earlier section.

Notes

[1] Ohmae, Kenichi (1982), *The Mind of the Strategist: The Art of Japanese Business.* New York, NY: McGraw-Hill.
[2] Adapted from Ibid.
[3] Asher, Mark and Eric Chung (2002), *Vault Guide to the Case Interview.* New York, NY: Vault Inc.
[4] Ohmae, Kenichi (1982), *The Mind of the Strategist: The Art of Japanese Business.* New York, NY: McGraw-Hill.
[5] Adapted from Ibid.

5.3. The S-T-P Framework

Snapshot: Segmentation, targeting, positioning

Overview: Segmentation-Targeting-Positioning (S-T-P) was introduced by Phillip Kotler as a universal approach to identify target customers and develop a distinct positioning of the offering in a customer's mind.[1] The S-T-P framework implies that the process of delivering customer value involves three key decisions: segmentation, targeting, and positioning (Figure 5.4). Segmenting the market, identifying target customers, and positioning the offering is an iterative process in which the company attempts to identify the customers who are most likely to benefit from its offering and develops a distinct image of the offering in the minds of these customers.

Figure 5.4. The S-T-P Framework

The first step, dividing customers into segments (or segmentation), is a subjective process in which the company groups customers with similar characteristics (e.g., needs, age, income, etc.). The process of segmentation is based on the idea that since customers in a given segment respond in a similar manner to a company's offerings, these customers can be treated as if they were a single entity and their needs can be served by the same offerings. Thus, through segmentation, the company can better manage the heterogeneity in the marketplace by focusing on a relatively small number of segments. Note that dividing the marketplace into separate segments is highly subjective and is likely to vary depending on the segmentation criterion. A good segmentation should yield segments that are mutually exclusive and collectively exhaustive: They should be sufficiently different from one another so that they do not overlap; at the same time they should account for all possible outcomes.

The second step, targeting, involves selecting which segment(s) to serve and which to ignore. When selecting target segments, the company's goal is to identify customers for whom it can deliver value superior to the competition in a way that allows the company and its collaborators to achieve their strategic goals.

The third step, positioning, involves creating a distinct image of a company's offering in its customers' minds.[2] Positioning reflects how the company wants its offering to be perceived and remembered by the customer; it is the process of creating a distinct image of the company's offering in a customer's mind. Because positioning involves prioritizing an offering's existing benefits and costs in order to highlight its key distinctive benefits, the same offering can often be positioned in multiple ways.

Limitations: One potential limitation of the S-T-P framework is that one of its key components – positioning – reflects only one aspect of an offering's value proposition. Whereas the value proposition captures *all* of the benefits and costs associated with a given offering, positioning captures only the *most distinct aspects* of a company's value proposition. By focusing solely on the most distinct aspects of a given offering rather than on its entire value proposition, the S-T-P approach offers a somewhat narrow view of customer value.

Notes

---

[1] Kotler, Philip (1984), *Marketing Management: Analysis, Planning, and Control* (5th ed.). Englewood Cliffs, NJ: Prentice-Hall.
[2] Ries, Al and Jack Trout (2001), *Positioning: The Battle for Your Mind* (20th anniversary ed.). New York, NY: McGraw-Hill.

5.4. The Value-Chain Framework

Snapshot: A systematic approach to examining the value delivery process

Overview: Value-chain analysis uses a descriptive approach to identify a sequence of functional elements in the process of value creation. Based on the level of generality and the underlying assumptions, there are different approaches to value-chain analysis.

One of the most popular frameworks for value-chain analysis is the one introduced by Michael Porter.[1] It distinguishes between two types of activities: primary activities and support activities (Figure 5.5). Primary activities are directly concerned with the creation or delivery of a product or service. They can be grouped into five main areas: inbound logistics (includes receiving, storing, inventory control, transportation scheduling); operations (machining, packaging, assembly, equipment maintenance, testing and all other value-creating activities that transform the inputs into the final product); outbound logistics (activities required to get the finished product to customers (warehousing, order fulfillment, transportation, distribution management); marketing and sales (activities associated with getting buyers to purchase the product, including channel selection, advertising, promotion, selling, pricing, retail management, etc.); and service (activities that maintain and enhance the product's value, including customer support, repair services, installation, training, spare parts management, upgrading, etc.).

Figure 5.5. The Value-Delivery Analysis: A Company Perspective[2]

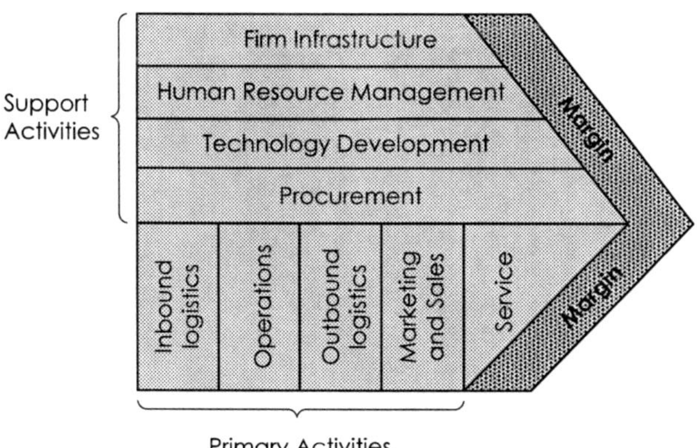

Each of these primary activities is linked to support activities that help improve their effectiveness or efficiency. There are four main areas of support activities: procurement (raw materials, servicing, spare parts, buildings, machines, etc.); technology development (e.g., research and development, process automation, design); human resource management (e.g., recruiting, development, retention and compensation of employees and managers); and infrastructure (e.g., general management, planning management, legal, finance, accounting, quality management).

A more general approach to analyzing the value-chain delivery process is to examine the value added by each member along the supply and distribution chains, as shown in Figure 5.6. The goal of this analysis is to optimize value creation by maximizing benefits while minimizing costs for each of the channel members, as well as across different channel members.

Figure 5.6. The Value-Delivery Process: An Industry Perspective

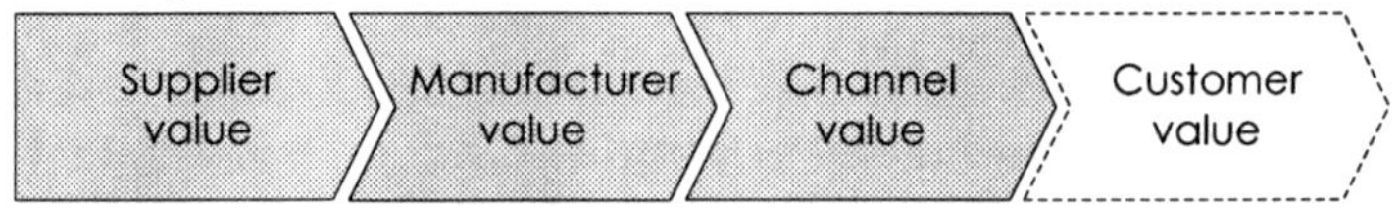

Application: The value-chain analysis is a useful tool for understanding the nature of the value-delivery process and optimizing the process by removing potential inefficiencies.

Notes

[1] Porter, Michael E. (1985), *Competitive Advantage: Creating and Sustaining Superior Performance*. New York: Free Press.

[2] Adapted from Ibid.

5.5. The 7-S Framework

Snapshot: Strategy, skills, shared values, structure, staff, systems, style

Overview: The basic idea of identifying several core factors that allow evaluating the effectiveness of an organization first appeared in *The Art of Japanese Management*[1] and was later introduced as the McKinsey 7-S Framework in Peters and Waterman's bestseller *In Search of Excellence.*[2] The 7-S framework involves analyzing seven interdependent aspects of a firm: strategy; skills (institutional capabilities such as the distinctive capabilities of personnel); shared values (culture – what the organization stands for and its central beliefs); structure (organization – the way the company's units relate to one another); staff (people – types of personnel within the organization, management training); systems (procedures – financial systems, information systems, as well as hiring, promotion and performance appraisal systems); and style (leadership style – how key managers work toward achieving the organization's goals). Working synergistically, these key factors account for the effectiveness of an organization. In this context, the 7-S framework calls for evaluating the seven key organizational factors and analyzing the relationships among them to ensure consistency (Figure 5.7).

Figure 5.7. 7-S Framework[3]

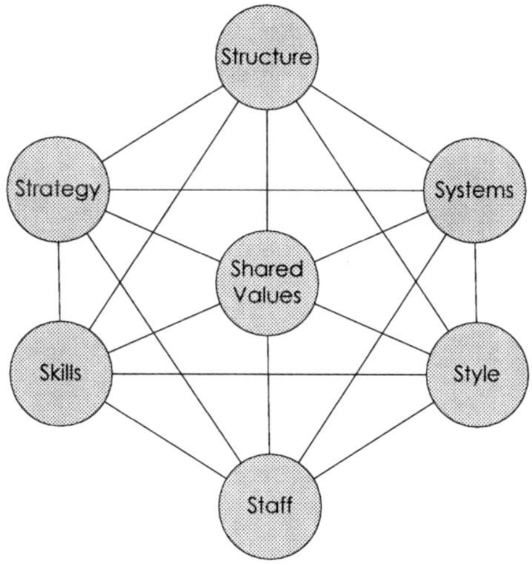

Application: McKinsey's 7-S framework is a very useful approach for analyzing the internal effectiveness and efficiency of an organization.

Notes

---

[1] Pascale, Richard T. and Anthony G. Athos (1981), *The Art of Japanese Management: Applications for American Executives.* New York, NY: Simon and Schuster.
[2] Adapted from Peters, Thomas J. and Robert H. Waterman (1982), *In Search of Excellence: Lessons from America's Best-Run Companies.* Cambridge: Harper & Row.
[3] Adapted from Ibid.

5.6. The BCG Product-Portfolio Framework

Snapshot: A 2 x 2 matrix for classifying and managing a company's strategic business units – stars (hold), question marks (build), cash cow (harvest), dogs (divest)

Overview: The BCG product-portfolio model is based on the notion that to be successful a company should have a portfolio of products with different market shares and different growth rates. The portfolio composition is viewed as a function of balancing cash flows between high-growth and low-growth products. In this context, the main goal of the BCG product portfolio model is to guide the cash-allocation decisions across different strategic business units (SBUs) of a company.

The BCG model is based on two key assumptions. The first assumption is that profit margins are a function of market share, such that high market share leads to high margins. This assumption is derived from the experience curve effect and, in particular, from the notion that increasing the scale of production leads to a lower cost structure and, hence, to higher profit margins.[1] The second assumption is that profit margins are a function of the growth of the industry in which the company operates and that different stages of growth require different cash-management strategies. In particular, high-growth businesses require cash investment, whereas low-growth businesses tend to generate cash in excess of what needs to be reinvested to maintain share. These two assumptions are reflected in the fact that market share and market growth are the two key components of evaluating the performance of a given strategic business unit.

Using the BCG matrix entails two major steps: classification and action. The *classification phase* calls for categorizing all SBUs into four types: question marks, stars, cash cows, and dogs. This categorization is based on each SBU's performance on two factors: (1) relative market share (share relative to the largest competitor) and (2) market growth. For example, a relative market share of 0.4 means that the SBU has 40% of the market leader's share, and a relative market share of 2.0 means that the SBU is the leader and has twice the share of the next largest competitor (Figure 5.8). For presentation purposes, the relative market share is drawn on a logarithmic scale. Market growth rate is drawn on a normal scale, with 10% annual market growth often used as the reference point.

Figure 5.8. BCG Matrix Step 1 (classification)[2]

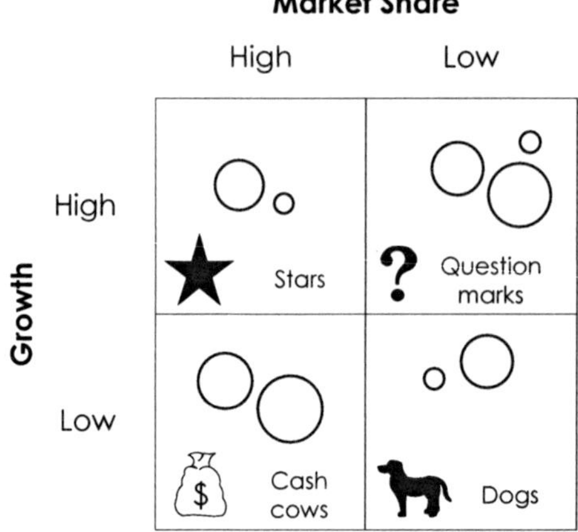

The *action phase* identifies the role to be assigned to each SBU (Figure 5.9). There are four basic strategies to achieve an efficient resource allocation: (1) Hold (preserve market share, usually applied to "stars"); (2) Build (increase market share and forgo near-term earnings, usually applied to "question marks"); (3) Harvest (increase cash flow and forgo building market share, usually applied to "cash cows"); and (4) Divest (sell or liquidate, usually applied to "dogs").

Figure 5.9. BCG Matrix: Step 2 (action)[3]

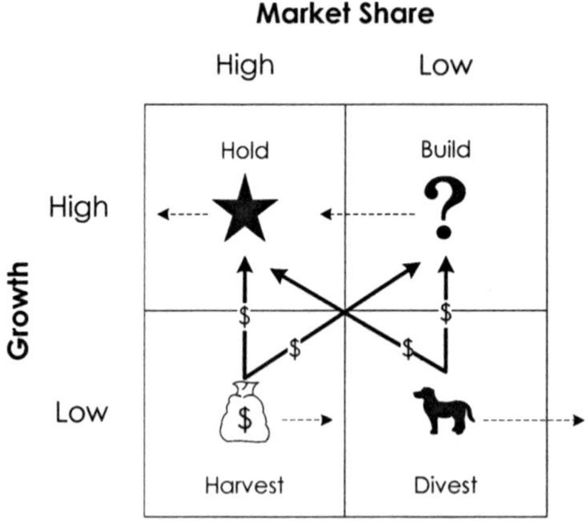

Limitations: The BCG model has numerous limitations. First, its main objective is to guide a company's resource allocation across different SBUs; as a result, it is not designed to assist with strategic decisions of a single SBU. Second, it considers market share and market growth to be the only relevant cash-allocation factors (factors such as cost, competitive reaction, synergies between SBUs, and various macroeconomic factors are not a part of the model). Third, it assumes that higher market share means higher cash-generating ability and higher profitability due to economies of scale, learning curve/experience effects, monopoly power, etc., even though these factors may not apply to all industries. Fourth, market share and market growth are ambiguous and difficult to quantify. To illustrate, the same SBU can be classified as a question mark, a star, a cash cow, or a dog when alternative operational definitions of the matrix dimensions are involved. Finally, the use of the BCG matrix can have important self-fulfilling organizational implications: Labeling an SBU as a dog will lead to minimizing the cash allocated to this unit, which is likely to decrease its performance and turn the unit into a real "dog."

Application: The BCG model offers a simple strategy for evaluating the relative performance of a company's strategic business units and making cash-allocation recommendations. Its recommendations, however, are based on highly restrictive assumptions (e.g., market share and industry growth rate are the only relevant performance factors), and its application is subject to multiple interpretations (e.g., defining the industry in which the firm competes). While the general idea of classifying a company's strategic business units based on their relative performance and the attractiveness of the industry in which they compete is a viable approach, the use of the BCG model in its original form in today's business world is rather limited.

Notes

---

[1] Stern, Carl W. and George Stalk (1998), *Perspectives on Strategy: From the Boston Consulting Group.* New York, NY: J. Wiley.

[2] Adapted from Ibid.

[3] Adapted from Ibid.

5.7. The GE Product-Portfolio Framework

Snapshot: A 3 x 3 matrix for classifying and managing a company's strategic business units

Overview: The GE product-portfolio model can be viewed as a more comprehensive version of the BCG model. Similar to the BCG model, it classifies business units into different categories based on their performance on two key business dimensions: market attractiveness and business strength (Figure 5.10). However, unlike the BCG matrix, where the dimensions are identified by a single factor (industry growth and market share), the GE matrix uses composite measures comprised of different factors. Thus, market attractiveness is calculated as a weighted average of factors such as market size, market growth, historical profit margin, stage in the life cycle, competitive intensity (number of competitors, competitive structure, differentiation, entry barriers, substitutes), technological requirements, inflationary vulnerability, investment intensity, and various context factors (e.g., social, political, and legal). In the same vein, business position is calculated as a weighted average of factors such as market share, share growth, product differentiation, brand image, relative cost position, capacity utilization, technological and R&D performance, patents, distribution network, marketing effectiveness, access to supplies, and managerial personnel.

Figure 5.10. GE Product-Portfolio Matrix

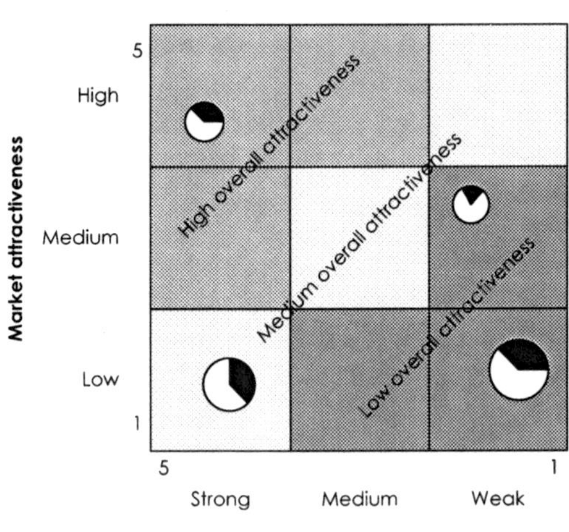

Because each of the two dimensions has three levels (low, medium, high), different strategic business units are classified into nine different types (rather than four, as in the BCG matrix). Each SBU is denoted with a circle representing the relative size of the market and the SBU's share of that market. The recommendations derived from the GE matrix are similar to that of the BCG approach, with the four key strategies further refined to match the 3 x 3 design of the GE matrix.

Limitations: The GE approach requires relatively complex analysis, which tends to limit its usability as a standardized approach. Similar to the BCG matrix, the GE approach suffers from subjectivity in evaluating different performance benchmarks (e.g., product differentiation, stage in the life cycle, brand image) and does not incorporate multi-period competitive strategies.

Application: The GE approach offsets many of the shortcomings of the BCG model – mainly its single-factor approach to identifying the key business factors that account for the overall profitability of a strategic business unit. This comprehensiveness, however, comes at the expense of simplicity, which is one of the most attractive features of the BCG matrix. Because of its complexity, the GE approach is often used as a guideline for analyzing different strategic business units rather than as a quantifiable normative model.

5.8. The 4-P Framework

Snapshot: Product, price, promotion, place

Overview: The 4-P model, introduced by Jerome McCarthy, offers a tool for planning and analyzing the implementation of a given marketing strategy.[1] According to this model, there are four key decisions that managers must make with respect to a given offering: what features to include in the product, how to price and promote the product, and in which distribution channels to "place" the product. These four decisions, often referred to as the marketing mix, are captured by the four P's: product, price, promotion, and place (Figure 5.11).

Figure 5.11. The 4-P Framework

Common Misconceptions: Most misinterpretations of the 4-P framework arise when managers try to fit different factors into the framework and focus on finding a factor starting with "p" rather than on the underlying logic. To illustrate, a common misinterpretation of the four P's involves adding positioning, people, or personnel as one of the P's. Positioning is not a marketing mix variable; rather, it is part of a company's overall strategy, which is then implemented through a particular combination of the marketing mix variables. In the same vein, people and personnel are typically viewed as an integral part of the company, rather than as a part of an offering's marketing mix. Another common misinterpretation of the 4-P framework concerns the use of "placement" instead of "place." Note that the term "placement" is commonly used in reference to a promotional strategy that involves embedding a product in various forms of entertainment.

Limitations: The first and most obvious limitation is the absence of separate service and image (brand) components in the 4-P model. Indeed, because it was developed to explain the process involved in marketing consumer-packaged goods, the 4-P model does not explicitly account for the service element of the offering – a key drawback in today's service-oriented business environment. Furthermore, the 4-P model does not explicitly consider the brand as a separate marketing mix variable. Instead, the brand is viewed as a part of a company's product and/or promotion decisions.

Another potential problem concerns the term "promotion." Promotion is a very broad term that includes two distinct types of marketing variables: incentives (e.g., price promotions, coupons, dealer incentives) and communications (e.g., advertising, public relations). While it is a common accounting practice to combine these factors, they each have a distinct impact on business processes; hence, for the purposes of strategic analysis, they should be considered independently from one another.

Finally, the use of the term "place" as an element of the marketing mix can be questioned, as well. As the process of delivering the company's offering to customers becomes increasingly complex, it is more accurate to refer to this process as "distribution" or "channel" rather than simply as "place." In fact, the term "place" is rarely used in business analysis.

Reconceptualization: Despite its limitations, the basic concept underlying the 4-P framework is logical and can be interpreted in context of the strategic marketing framework outlined earlier in this book. In this context, the product and the price can be viewed as a representation of the benefits and costs in the process of creating value; promotions can be viewed as a representation of the communications aspect; and finally, the place can be viewed as a representation of the value-delivery process (Figure 5.12).

Figure 5.12. Reconceptualizing the Four P's

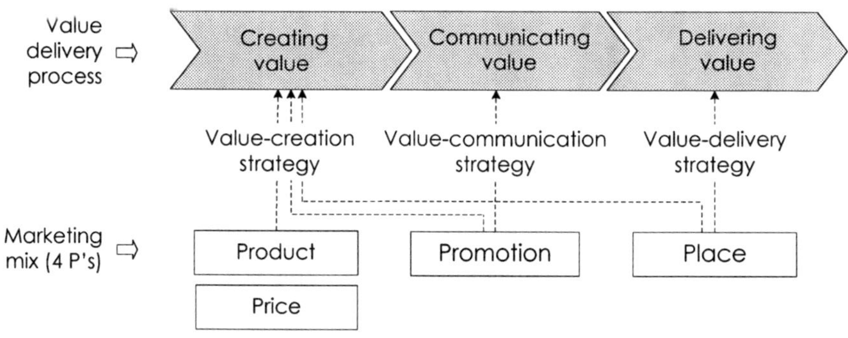

Application: The 4-P framework offers an overview of the key decision variables involved in the implementation of a given marketing strategy. Because of its limitations, however, business analysis can be better served by a more comprehensive and up-to-date framework.

Notes

---

[1] McCarthy, E. Jerome and William D. Perreault (1996), *Basic Marketing: A Managerial Approach* (12th ed.). Homewood, IL: Irwin.

5.9. Product Life Cycle Framework

Snapshot: Identifies four stages of a product life cycle: introduction, growth, maturity, and decline

Overview: The concept of a product life cycle introduced by Theodore Levitt[1] is based on four key assumptions: (1) products have a limited life, (2) they pass through distinct stages, (3) their profitability depends on the stage, and, as a result, (4) different stages require different marketing strategies (Figure 5.13). At the introduction stage, product awareness is low and there are very few competitors; hence the company's primary goal tends to be creating awareness and educating customers about the benefits of the product. As the product takes off during the growth stage, the number of competitors entering the market increases as well. In this context, the company's goal is likely to change from customer education to differentiation from the competition. At maturity, the number of competitors tends to peak, the market becomes saturated, and industry profitability starts to decline because of intensifying competition. Finally, the decline stage is characterized by declining demand for the product, relatively low profitability, and a decreasing number of competitors stemming from consolidation and/or exit from the market.

Figure 5.13. Product Life Cycle[2]

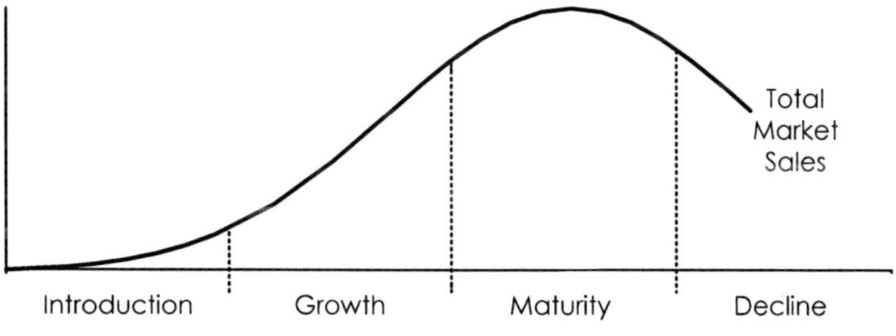

Limitations: The product life cycle framework is a descriptive tool used to illustrate the general trend of products as they go through different stages in the marketplace; it is not designed to predict the future market success of a particular product. The product life cycle framework does not predict exactly when a product switches from an introductory stage to a growth, maturity, and/or decline stage.

Application: The product life cycle framework describes the general trend of products and services as they progress through different stages in the marketplace. As such, it is an invaluable planning tool that allows managers to anticipate changes in the market environment and develop adaptive market strategies.

Notes

---

[1] Levitt, Theodore (1965), "Exploit the Product Life Cycle," *Harvard Business Review*, 43, (Nov/Dec), 81-94.
[2] Adapted from Ibid.

5.10. A-T-R Product Adoption Framework

Snapshot: Awareness, trial, and repeat

Overview: A-T-R is a product adoption framework according to which new product adoption goes through the following three stages: *awareness*, *trial* (purchase), and *repeat* purchase. The A-T-R framework is often used to evaluate and estimate the process of new product adoption. In this context, there are four key product adoption metrics derived from the A-T-R framework: awareness rate, conversion rate, penetration rate, and retention rate (Figure 5.14).

Figure 5.14: A-T-R Model

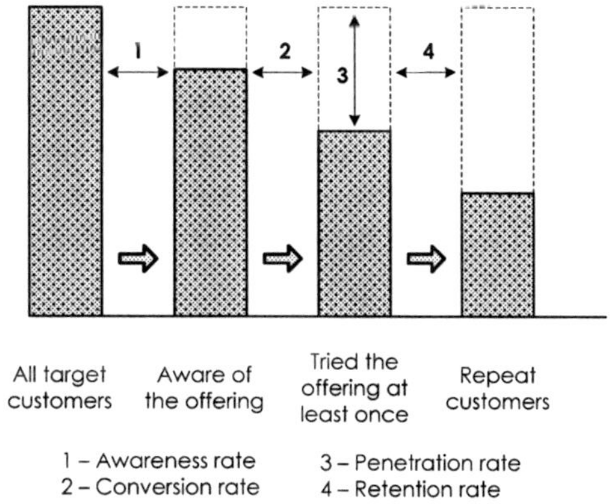

Awareness rate reflects the number of customers who are aware of the offering relative to the total number of potential customers. *Conversion rate* reflects the number of customers who have tried the product/service relative to the total number of customers aware of the product/service. *Penetration rate* is used to describe the number of customers who have tried the offering at least once relative to the total number of potential customers. Finally *retention rate* reflects the number of customers who have repurchased the offering during the current buying cycle (e.g., month, quarter, or year) relative to the number of customers who have purchased the offering during the last cycle.

Awareness, conversion, and retention rates can be used to identify potential problems in product adoption as shown in Figures 5.15 and 5.16.

Figure 5.15: Using the A-T-R Model to Identify Problems in Product Adoption: Low Trial Rates

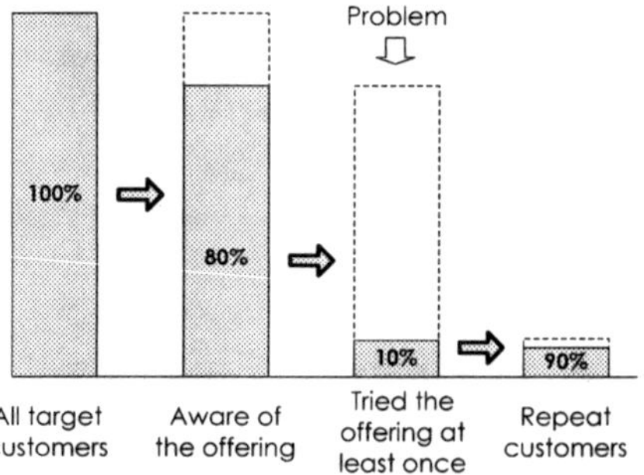

Figure 5.15 depicts a scenario in which an offering's inferior performance can be traced to the fact that despite the high awareness of the offering, very few customers have actually tried the offering. Nearly all of those who have tried the offering, however, have become repeat customers. In this context, the company's strategy should focus on converting the high product awareness into trials (e.g., by using incentives and broadening distribution).

The scenario shown in Figure 5.16 illustrates a case in which a company's inability to create a loyal customer base is caused by the inferiority of its offering. Indeed, only 10% of those who tried the offering decided to repurchase it – a fact that could be attributed to factors such as inferior product performance (e.g., poor design, inadequate functionality, not user-friendly), high price, and lack of repeat-customer incentives. In this context, the company's strategy should focus on retaining its existing customers (e.g., by improving a product's performance, introducing loyalty programs).

Figure 5.16: Using the A-T-R Model to Identify Problems in Product Adoption: Low Offering Attractiveness

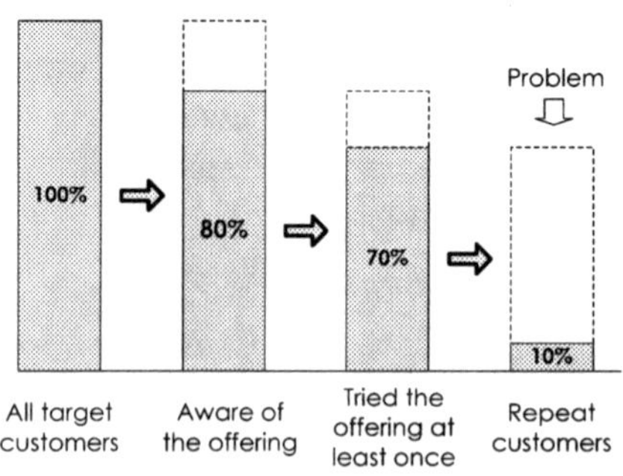

Awareness, conversion, and retention rates can also be used to estimate the size of an offering's customer base as follows:

Customer base = Target customers * Conversion rate * Retention rate

Application: The A-T-R framework is a very useful approach for planning new offerings and estimating their market potential. The A-T-R framework is also often used for segmentation purposes to devise customer-specific marketing strategies based on the stage of the customer in the product-adoption cycle (e.g., new vs. repeat customers).

5.11. Push-Pull Promotions Framework

Snapshot: Promotion management framework comprising two distinct promotion strategies: push and pull

Overview: Push strategy describes the practice of creating demand for a company's offering by promoting the offering through incentives and communications to channel members, who in turn push the product downstream to end-users (Figure 5.17). To illustrate, the manufacturer might offer high margins on their products and services so that retailers have a vested interest in selling the product. In the same vein, the manufacturer might educate retailers' sales force about the benefits of its offerings and provide the retailer with promotional materials, thus facilitating the sales process.

Figure 5.17. Push Strategy

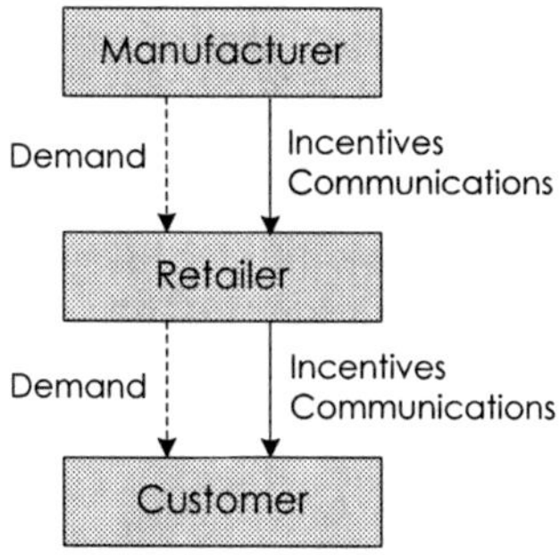

Manufacturer

Demand | Incentives Communications

Retailer

Demand | Incentives Communications

Customer

The pull strategy, in contrast, refers to the practice of creating demand for a company's offering by promoting the offering directly to end-users, who in turn demand the offering from retailers, ultimately "pulling" the offering through the channel (Figure 5.18). To illustrate, the manufacturer might extensively advertise its products and services to the end-users and/or promote its offerings through direct mail, coupons, contests, etc.

Figure 5.18. Pull Strategy

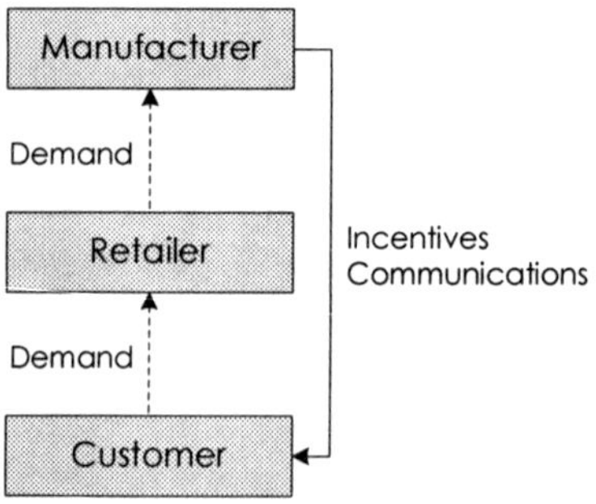

In addition to using either of these strategies in isolation, a company can use a push-pull strategy that combines the characteristics of both push and pull strategies. Combining the elements of a promotional push and pull ensures greater marketing effectiveness, which often justifies the increased marketing costs since promotions are now channeled to both customers and distributors.

Application: The push-pull promotion framework is a useful tool for understanding and optimizing the effectiveness of promotional resources associated with a given offering.

5.12. A-I-D-A Communications Framework

Snapshot: Attention, interest, desire, action

Overview: A-I-D-A is a framework of consumer decision-making used to illustrate the process of converting advertising to sales. A derivation of an earlier framework conceptualizing advertising as a process of attention, comprehension, and understanding,[1] the A-I-D-A framework posits that the consumer decision process involves four key steps: attention, interest, desire, and action[2] (Figure 5.19). A hierarchical effects framework, A-I-D-A posits that before making a purchase decision consumers need to be made *aware* that the offering exists and be stimulated to take some *interest* in the offering. Then, a *desire* must be created among consumers to purchase the offering, which must be translated into *action* that leads to the actual purchase of the offering. The A-I-D-A framework calls for developing focused communication strategies depending on which stage of the decision process target customers are in.

Figure 5.19. A-I-D-A Communications Framework

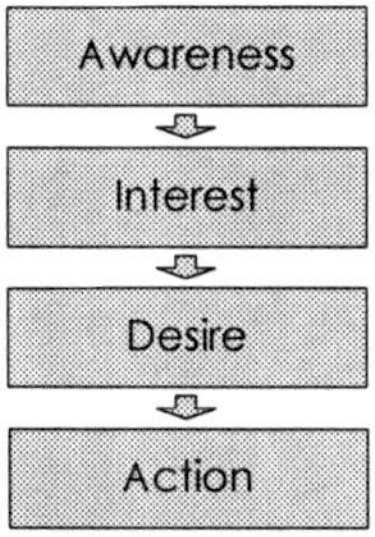

Limitations: One of the key limitations of the A-I-D-A framework is that customers' decision processes are unobservable and, as a result, it is often impossible to identify the decision stage for a given customer. In addition, many purchase decisions (e.g., impulsive purchases) do not follow the four-stage attention-interest-desire-action decision process.

Application: A-I-D-A is an intuitive representation of consumer decision making used to guide advertising decisions by linking the particular stage in consumer decision process to specific communication strategies.

Notes

---

[1] Scott, Walter Dill (1913), *The Psychology of Advertising*. Boston, MA: Small Maynard.

[2] Lavidge, Robert J. and Gary A. Steiner (1961), "A Model for Predictive Measurements of Advertising Effectiveness," *Journal of Marketing*, 25, (6), 59-62.

Author Profile

Alexander Chernev is associate professor of marketing at the Kellogg School of Management, Northwestern University, where he teaches the core marketing management course to MBA students and behavioral decision theory to Ph.D. students. He holds a Ph.D. in Psychology from Sofia University and a Ph.D. in Business Administration from Duke University. Professor Chernev's research applies theories and concepts related to consumer behavior and managerial decision making to develop successful corporate branding and customer management strategies. His research has been published in leading marketing journals, and he has received numerous teaching and research awards. Professor Chernev serves on the editorial boards of the top research journals and has advised numerous companies on issues such as strategic marketing, new product development, and customer management policies. Professor Chernev has provided career advice to numerous students, many of whom are currently working for Fortune 500 companies and others who are in the process of building their own Fortune 500 companies.

Printed in the United States
53826LVS00001B/268-285

9 780976 306177